MOLECULES, MEASUREMENTS, MEANINGS

MOLECULES, MEASUREMENTS, MEANINGS

A LABORATORY MANUAL IN BIOCHEMISTRY

David W. Krogmann
Purdue University

W. H. FREEMAN AND COMPANY
San Francisco

International Standard Book Number: 0-7167-0156-1

9 8 7 6 5 4 3 2 1

ACKNOWLEDGMENTS

I am grateful to John Christopher, Michael Rogers, and Flora Mao for their help in the design and testing of these experiments. Dr. Ki-Han Kim gave generously of his time and skill in the design of several of these experiments. The excellent work of Carolyn Swan in preparing the manuscript is a pleasure to acknowledge. Thanks are especially due to Loretta Krogmann for her careful reading of this manuscript and for many helpful suggestions.

March 1971   *David W. Krogmann*

CONTENTS

TO THE STUDENT

Biochemistry is a relatively new science, and the experiments in this manual are intended to illustrate both the underlying chemistry of some biological phenomena and the immediate relevance of this science to contemporary experience. It seems to me you should find biochemistry to be intrinsically fascinating—its main object of study is, after all, life, a subject in which everyone shares a certain egocentric interest. Furthermore, life is dealt with here in the esthetically pleasing modes of precision, color, symmetry, and shape. We are witnessing both a golden age of biological discovery and an era of social development in which the biological and chemical alterations of our environment have enormous importance. The primary justification of these laboratory exercises is to help you to see the facts, principles, and operational activities of biochemistry—to see them better, to see them from a different angle, possibly to think about them as they will apply to the daily affairs of men. Everyone these days must make judgments about the use of pesticides, the alteration of foods, the use of drugs and medicines. Such judgments should be based on experimental realities, and hence these exercises may have more than "academic" value.

For each of the major classes of biological molecules, there are several experiments in this manual, arranged in the following sequence: (a) procedures for separating mixtures of molecules into individual types, and identifing the chemical characteristics of each type; (b) a model-building session to illustrate the three-dimensional reality of the molecule and the physical basis for its properties; (c) observations of the dynamic properties of the molecules as they operate in living systems. These experiments, then, represent three biochemical approaches to living processes. The isolation, chemical description, and elucidation of the three-dimensional structure of DNA, an extremely complex biological molecule, are a triumph of our time, and the techniques used to accomplish this feat appear to be applicable in principle to the description of all molecules. The relation of molecular structure to biological activity is less clear, and this clarification will be a challenge in the future.

In addition to your text and the references given in these experiments, there are other sources of biochemical background that can be enjoyed in less formal settings. On the paperback bookstands in almost any bus station or drugstore, you might find the following important and readable works:

Arrowsmith, Sinclair Lewis (Signet),
Microbe Hunters, Paul DeKruif (Pocket Books);
Silent Spring, Rachel Carson (Fawcett Crest);
The Two Cultures, C. P. Snow (Mentor);
The Andromeda Strain, M. Crichton (Dell)
Mushrooms, Molds, and Miracles, L. Kavaler (Signet);
The Incurable Wound, Breton Roche (Berkeley);
The Double Helix, J. D. Watson (Signet).

SOME GENERAL NOTES ON THE PRESERVATION OF EXPERIMENTS AND EXPERIMENTERS

Experiment number four reveals several conditions—extremes of acid, alkali, heat, etc.—that destroy enzyme activity. Since vital processes depend on enzymes, you might expect that these extreme conditions will also destroy living cells, organisms, even experimenters. In consequence, there are some rules. Never pipette strong acids and bases, but instead dispense them from a burette, to avoid the risk of getting them in your mouth. As a general rule, enzyme inhibitors are toxic to humans; so treat them with respect. As in many things, the quantity is important. In experiment four, fluoride ion is seen to inhibit an enzyme, but in a concentration several millionfold higher than is frequently added to drinking water to prevent tooth decay. Eating or smoking in a laboratory is *out*, because you *might* get an enzyme inhibitor on the sandwich or cigarette. Conversely, don't spill mustard in an enzyme preparation, or stir the experiment with a glass rod that has been lying on the bench top. The last class may have soaked the bench top with copper sulfate. Likewise, if the glassware isn't clean, wash it or cut class, because the experiment won't mean much if it is done in a dirty test tube.

A point of technique that is most frequently overlooked in doing experiments such as these is that reagents need to be mixed. Diffusion is too slow a process to depend on in a three-hour lab; you can't wait for the reagents to mix themselves. The contents of a test tube are easily mixed by holding the tube near the top between the thumb and forefinger, and striking the bottom of the tube with the forefinger of the free hand.

In using pipettes, always check the top of the pipette for chips, lest you get a cut lip. Your instructor will demonstrate the use of the pipette. Always hold the pipette between the thumb and second finger, using the forefinger, not the thumb, to control the liquid level. Don't pipette the last few drops out of a container, since doing so often gets the experiment in your mouth.

Finally, take notes. Numerical data must be recorded, and recorded in such a way that you can reconstruct the experiment and its meaning later on. The process of gathering data in a busy laboratory is not always conducive to understanding fully the meanings of those data; so record both the numbers and where they came from, on something less likely to be discarded than a paper towel. In making graphs, observe the convention of plotting the experimentally obtained values (dependent variable) on the vertical axis or ordinate. The independent variable, such as time, wavelength, or amount of enzyme, should be plotted on the horizontal axis or abcissa. This is an arbitrary but universally used convention, which saves everyone a lot of time in looking at graphs, since they automatically know where to find things. It is like driving on the righthand side of the street: without the convention, you must go more slowly, and the chances for error are greater.

DAVID W. KROGMANN

MOLECULES, MEASUREMENTS, MEANINGS

AMINO ACIDS, THE BUILDING BLOCKS OF PROTEINS

Separation of Complex Mixtures of Amino Acids and Recognition of Individual Chemical Properties

The purpose of this experiment is to acquaint you with the twenty amino acids found in all living things, and with the differences among them. In order to study any member of a class, one must first separate the member from all the others in the class and recognize that member's individual characteristics. The class of amino acids must be sorted into its twenty individual members. Such sorting is conveniently done by paper chromatography. Each amino acid will migrate a characteristic distance across a paper, depending on its relative solubility in the two solvents used to irrigate the paper.

Individual amino acids may be recognized by the use of a reagent that reacts with only one amino acid, but not with any of the other nineteen. The reaction produces a color, and the intensity of the color is often a function of the amount of the amino acid present in a sample. Even the most subtle differences in the stereochemistry of amino acids can be detected by the use of an enzyme. For example, D-amino acid oxidase will react with only one of the two possible isomers of any amino acid.

EXPERIMENTAL PROCEDURES

1. Chromatographic Separation of Amino Acids

Various amino acids will move to different positions as an organic solvent moves across a water-saturated paper. You must use lead pencil in marking your chromatogram, since both ink and wax-pencil markings can be separated into component pigments by chromatography, making a mess of your amino acid separation experiment. On the chromatography paper provided, draw a pencil line ¾ of an inch from the long edge of the paper, and parallel to it. Then mark on it seven equally spaced points, leaving about half an inch of margin from each of the shorter edges. Number these points 1 through 7. Take care not to press your fingers against the paper, for your fingertips will leave amino acids. You will be given a series of seven amino acid solutions, each with a wooden applicator stick in it. At each of the seven pencil marks along the origin line, transfer the smallest pos-

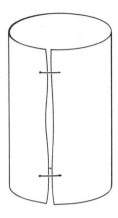

FIGURE 1.1.

Paper chromatogram stapled as a cylinder.

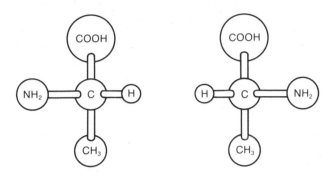

FIGURE 1.2.

Optical isomers of alanine, one of the 20-odd amino acids that link up to form proteins, illustrate what is meant by an "asymmetric" carbon atom. The central carbon is asymmetric because it has attached to each of its four chemical bonds a different kind of atom or group of atoms. When in solution one configuration, called L(−)-alanine (*left*), rotates plane-polarized light to the left; its mirror image, D(+)-alanine (*right*), rotates polarized light to the right. Natural proteins are all built from L(−)-amino acids. (From G. Natta, "Precisely Constructed Polymers." Copyright © 1961 by Scientific American, Inc. All rights reserved.)

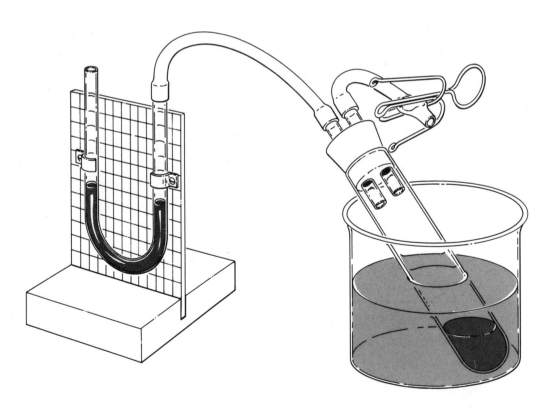

FIGURE 1.3.

∪-tube manometer.

sible drop of the amino acid solution with the corresponding number. Try to wet an area of the paper not more than twice the diameter of the applicator stick. Spot the solutions in the following order:

(1) casein hydrolysate,
(2) tyrosine,
(3) alanine,
(4) valine,
(5) proline,
(6) unknown,
(7) lysozyme.

Pencil your initials on the lower righthand corner of the paper. When the spots have dried, bend the paper into a cylinder and staple it together at the top and bottom so that the edges do not touch (see Figure 1.1).

In the hood you will find an 800-ml beaker covered with Saran Wrap, and containing 21 ml of *n*-propanol and 9 ml of concentrated ammonium hydroxide. (CAUTION: avoid the fumes or spillage). Initial the beaker and place your paper cylinder in it, with the spotted edge down in the solvent. Cover the beaker, and seal the Saran Wrap tightly with a rubber band.

When the solvent has risen to about half an inch from the top of the paper (45 to 60 minutes), remove the paper from the solvent, remove the staples, mark the solvent front with pencil, and spread the paper to dry on a paper towel.

When the solvent has evaporated, the instructor will help you spray the paper with ninhydrin. Dry the paper again, and then heat it in an 80°C oven for two minutes. Draw a circle around each spot formed.

2. Specific Reactions of Amino Acids

Often one must measure the quantity of one specific amino acid in a biological fluid containing many amino acids. One can test for the presence of arginine with the Sakaguchi reaction, or for the presence of the sulfhydryl group of cysteine with Ellman's reagent. To distinguish between the D and L isomers of an amino acid, one can use the stereospecific enzyme D-amino acid oxidase, which oxidizes only the D form.

a. Sakaguchi reaction. Put 5 ml of alanine, arginine, and lysozyme in different test tubes. Add from a burette 1 ml of NaOH solution and 1 ml of alpha napthol solution. Mix, then cool for 2 or 3 minutes in ice. Add 5 drops of NaOBr solution, and shake for 5 seconds. Red color means a positive test.

b. Ellman's reaction. Place 5 drops each of cysteine, methionine, lysozyme, casein, and water in different test tubes. Add 3 ml of "Tris" buffer, *p*H 8, from a burette to each tube, then add 1 ml of Ellman's reagent to each tube. Mix and wait 2 or 3 minutes. A bright yellow color is a positive test.

c. D-amino acid oxidase. This enzyme uses atmospheric oxygen to attack the D-stereoisomers of amino acids specifically (see Figure 1.2). Oxygen uptake is measured by following the decrease in atmospheric pressure in a closed system. Add 1 ml of D-alanine to a test tube, and stand it in a beaker of water for 5 minutes to let it reach temperature equilibrium. Add one drop of enzyme. Stopper the tube with the two-hole stopper attached to the manometer, then close the vent tube with a pinch clamp (see Figure 1.3). Note the level of the blue indicator fluid in the open arm of the ∪-tube, and continue to observe for ten minutes.

A ∪-tube manometer will respond to changes in gas pressure in the closed system. The indicator fluid will rise in the arm connected to the test tube if the gas pressure decreases—say, as a result of oxygen uptake. The fluid will drop if the gas pressure increases. Since the system is temperature-sensitive, you must keep the tube partially immersed in a beaker of water.

Connect the tube to the manometer, close the outlet vent with a pinch clamp, then hold the tube in your hand for several minutes. What effect does this have on the fluid height in the manometer? (Use the side connected to the test tube for all observations.) Why does the manometer register change?

3. Protein Amino Acid Mapping

In part 1 you developed a simple (i.e., 7-spot) chromatogram in (essentially) one dimension. But for the casein hydrolysate, in position number 1, the spots were not all well-separated. To separate a larger number of amino acids, the chromatogram can be taken out of the first solvent, dried, rotated through 90 degrees, and developed in a second dimension (see Figure 1.4). In the second solvent, the amino acids move to different relative positions compared to the first solvent, allowing the resolution of more individual amino acids. Since a protein may contain up to twenty amino acids, you need all the sorting out you can get. To identify all the amino acids in a protein, you must first hydrolyze it—break the peptide bonds by cooking it in strong acid until all the individual amino acids have been split from the polypeptide chain.

FIGURE 1.4.

Paper chromatography separates the 17 amino acids of insulin. In the chromatogram represented by this diagram, insulin was broken down by hydrolysis, and a sample of the mixture placed at the upper left on the sheet of paper. The sheet was hung from a trough filled with solvent, which carried each amino acid a characteristic distance down the paper. The sheet was then turned 90 degrees and the process repeated. The amino acids, with the exception of proline, appear as purple spots when sprayed with ninhydrin. (From E. O. P. Thompson, "The Insulin Molecule." Copyright © 1955 by Scientific American, Inc. All rights reserved.)

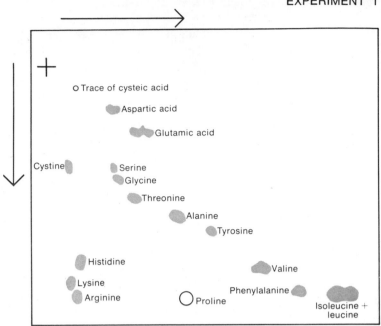

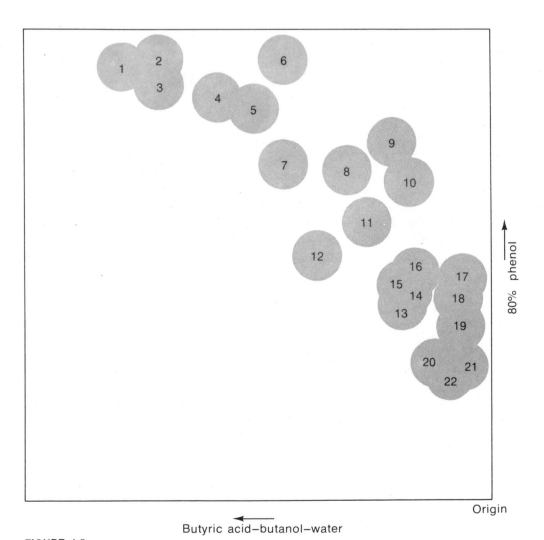

FIGURE 1.5.

Chromatogram "master map."

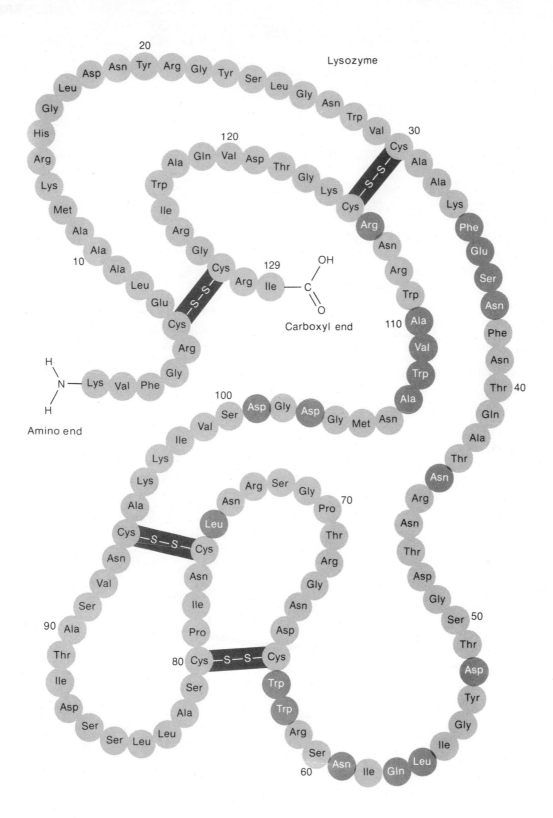

FIGURE 1.6.

The amino acid sequence of lysozyme. (From D. C. Phillips, "The Three-dimensional Structure of an Enzyme Molecule." Copyright © 1966 by Scientific American, Inc. All rights reserved.)

You will be given a two-dimensional chromatogram with one known amino acid on it. Spray it with ninhydrin, and develop the color. Identify the position of your amino acid on the master map hanging on the wall, and fill out your copy of the master map (Figure 1.5) with the location of all amino acids.

You will be given a real or facsimile two-dimensional chromatogram of a hydrolyzed protein. Spray it with ninhydrin, and heat it for 3 minutes to develop the color. Identify each of the spots from the master map, and label them.

NOTES AND REVIEW QUESTIONS

Chromatographic Separation

1. Report the R_f (i.e., the ratio of the distance traveled by the compound to the distance traveled by the solvent) for tyrosine, alanine, valine, and proline.
2. Is there any difference in the color produced by ninhydrin with these amino acids?
3. Which amino acid was present as the unknown at position 6?
4. What did the chromatogram tell you about the amino acid composition of the milk protein, casein?
5. What did your chromatogram tell you about the amino acid composition of the egg-white protein, lysozyme? Why did this differ from the casein result? (See Figure 1.6.)

Specific Reactions

6. Is the Sakaguchi reaction specific?

7. What does the Sakaguchi reaction reveal concerning the presence of arginine in lysozyme?
8. Why doesn't Ellman's reagent react the same way with the two sulfur amino acids, cysteine and methionine?
9. What does Ellman's reagent tell you about lysozyme and casein?
10. Why is it necessary to control the temperature when measuring the D-amino acid oxidase reaction?
11. If you were to hold the test tube clenched in your hand while it is attached to the manometer with the vent closed, what would happen to the fluid level in the open arm of the ∪-tube, and why?

Protein Mapping

12. Attach the chromatogram of the hydrolyzed protein sample with each of the spots identified. By referring to your text, comment on any unusual aspects of the amino acid composition of this protein.

REFERENCES

1. S. Aronoff, *Techniques of Radiobiochemistry* (Iowa State College Press, 1956). Chapter 9 is an excellent storehouse of information and techniques useful in the study of amino acids.
2. R. E. Dickerson and I. Geis, *The Structure and Action of Proteins* (Harper & Row, 1969).
3. W. H. Stein and S. Moore, "The Chemical Structure of Proteins," *Scientific American*, February 1961. Also available as Scientific American Offprint No. 80 (W. H. Freeman and Company).

PROTEIN STRUCTURE, AN ADDITIONAL DIMENSION

Models Illustrating Optical Isomerism, Amino Acid Sequence, and the Three-Dimensional Character of Protein Structure

> "This branch of science at present goes by the name of molecular biology. It begins with the analysis of crystal structure, itself a subject aesthetically beautiful and easily comprehended. It goes on to the application of these methods to molecules which have literally a vital part in our own existence—molecules of proteins, nucleic acids: molecules immensely large (by molecular standards)—and which turn out to be of curious shapes, for nature, when interested in what we call life, appears to have a taste for the rococo."
>
> C. P. Snow, *The Two Cultures: and a Second Look*

This experiment is meant to acquaint you with the physical dimensions of proteins and of their constituent amino acids, and with the arrangement of the parts within the whole. Since most amino acids contain an asymmetric alpha carbon, the models of the D- and L-isomers of an amino acid that you will build will show you the geometric basis of optical isomerism—a phenomenon that is encountered repeatedly in the study of organic compounds. Next, you will assemble a rather extensive model of the amino acid sequence of a protein, in order to see that proteins are a complicated but very precise assembly of amino acids. You should be able to see that a mistake in amino acid sequence is the chemical expression of a mutation, and that the sequence may vary when the same type of molecule is isolated from different species of animals. Finally, you will make a three-dimensional model of a protein, in order to acquire a more solid sense of how these molecules are structured.

EXPERIMENTAL PROCEDURES

1. Stereoisomers of an Amino Acid

Build models of D- and L-alanine with the atomic model sets, referring to Figure 1.2 as a guide. When you have completed the two models, sketch them to show their differences. Look at them in the mirror to see the "mirror image" relation. Compare these models with the other models of D- and L-amino acids on display in the lab.

2. Amino Acid Sequence of a Polypeptide Chain

You will be given a length of bare wire with a label attached to identify the polypeptide chain you are to assemble. The foam-rubber amino acid symbols to be used are identified by three letters (these are usually the first three letters of the name of the amino acid), and very roughly approximate the shape of the amino acids (see Figure 2.1). Align the symbols, with the printed side parallel to the long axis of the wire, by passing the wire through the base piece, which is common to all the symbols. Write your name on the label tag and have the instructor check the sequence for accuracy. Set aside your model until the end of the period, when all the models can be discussed with the entire class. Assemble a model of ribonuclease (see Figure 2.3), and note how the disulfide bridges impose new constraints on the structure of the protein. You should link the appropriate cysteine residues together with short lengths of wire.

FIGURE 2.1.
Amino acid symbols.

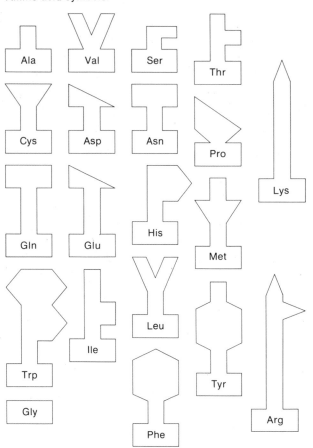

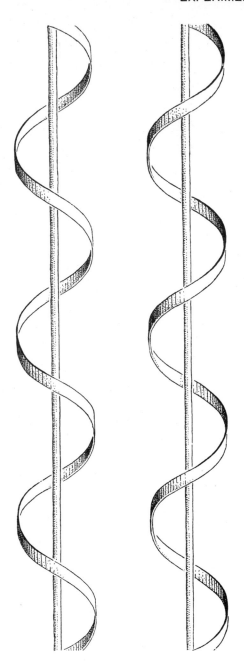

FIGURE 2.2.
Asymmetry of a helix is either left-handed (left) or right-handed. Helix in proteins appears to be exclusively right-handed. (From P. Doty, "Proteins." Copyright © 1957 by Scientific American, Inc. All rights reserved.)

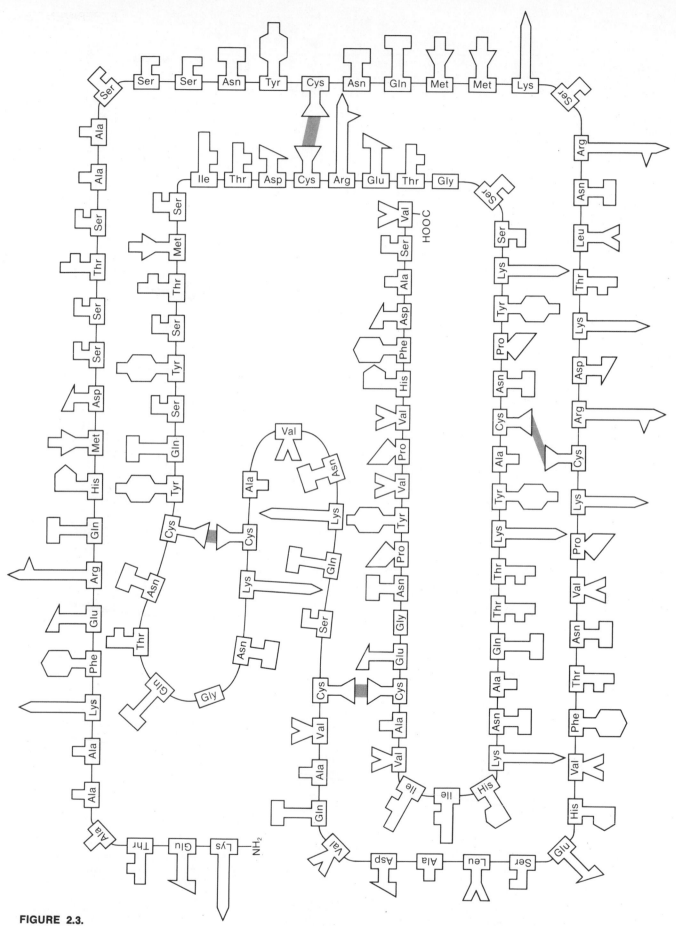

FIGURE 2.3.

The amino acid sequence of insulin.

Hemoglobin chains

Residues 1–36

Chain	1	2	3	4	5	6	7	8	9	10	11	12	13	14	15	16	17	18	19	20	21	22	23	24	25	26	27	28	29	30	31	32	33	34	35	36
Human-Beta	Val	His	Leu	Thr	Pro	Glu	Glu	Lys	Ser	Ala	Val	Thr	Ala	Leu	Trp	Gly	Lys	Val	Asn	Val	Asp	Glu	Val	Gly	Gly	Glu	Ala	Leu	Gly	Arg	Leu	Leu	Val	Val	Tyr	P
Human-Delta	Val	His	Leu	Thr	Pro	Glu	Glu	Lys	Thr	Ala	Val	Asn	Ala	Leu	Trp	Gly	Lys	Val	Asn	Val	Asp	Ala	Val	Gly	Gly	Glu	Ala	Leu	Gly	Arg	Leu	Leu	Val	Val	Tyr	P
Human-Gamma	Gly	His	Phe	Thr	Glu	Glu	Asp	Lys	Ala	Thr	Ile	Thr	Ser	Leu	Trp	Gly	Lys	Val	Asn	Val	Glu	Asp	Ala	Gly	Gly	Glu	Thr	Leu	Gly	Arg	Leu	Leu	Val	Val	Tyr	P
Human-Alpha	Val	Leu	Ser	Pro	Ala	Asp	Lys	Thr	Asn	Val	Lys	Ala	Ala	Trp	Gly	Lys	Val	Gly	Ala	His	Ala	Gly	Glu	Tyr	Gly	Ala	Glu	Ala	Leu	Glu	Arg	Met	Phe	Leu	Ser	Phe
Gorilla-Beta	Val	His	Leu	Thr	Pro	Glu	Glu	Lys	Ser	Ala	Val	Thr	Ala	Leu	Trp	Gly	Lys	Val	Asn	Val	Asp	Glu	Val	Gly	Gly	Glu	Ala	Leu	Gly	Arg	Leu	Leu	Val	Val	Tyr	P
Pig-Beta	Val	His	Leu	Ser	Ala	Glu	Glu	Lys	Ser	Ala	Val	Thr	Ala	Leu	Trp	Gly	Lys	Val	Asn	Val	Asp	Glu	Val	Gly	Gly	Glu	Ala	Leu	Gly	Arg	Leu	Leu	Val	Val	Tyr	P
Horse-Beta	Val	Gln	Leu	Ser	Gly	Glu	Glu	Lys	Ala	Ala	Val	Leu	Ala	Leu	Trp	Asp	Lys	Val	Asn	Glu	Glu	Glu	Val	Gly	Gly	Glu	Ala	Leu	Gly	Arg	Leu	Leu	Val	Val	Tyr	P
Whale myoglobin	Val	Leu	Ser	Glu	Gly	Glu	Trp	Gln	Leu	Val	Leu	His	Val	Trp	Ala	Lys	Val	Glu	Ala	Asp	Val	Ala	Gly	His	Gly	Gln	Asp	Ile	Leu	Ile	Arg	Leu	Phe	Lys	Ser	His

Residues 76–113

Chain	76	77	78	79	80	81	82	83	84	85	86	87	88	89	90	91	92	93	94	95	96	97	98	99	100	101	102	103	104	105	106	107	108	109	110	111	112
Human-Beta	Ala	His	Leu	Asp	Asn	Leu	Lys	Gly	Thr	Phe	Ala	Thr	Leu	Ser	Glu	Leu	His	Cys	Asp	Lys	Leu	His	Val	Asp	Pro	Glu	Asn	Phe	Arg	Leu	Leu	Gly	Asn	Val	Leu	Val	Cys
Human-Delta	Ala	His	Leu	Asp	Asn	Leu	Lys	Gly	Thr	Phe	Ser	Gln	Leu	Ser	Glu	Leu	His	Cys	Asp	Lys	Leu	His	Val	Asp	Pro	Glu	Asn	Phe	Arg	Leu	Leu	Gly	Asn	Val	Leu	Val	Cys
Human-Gamma	Lys	His	Leu	Asp	Asp	Leu	Lys	Gly	Thr	Phe	Ala	Gln	Leu	Ser	Glu	Leu	His	Cys	Asp	Lys	Leu	His	Val	Asp	Pro	Glu	Asn	Phe	Lys	Leu	Leu	Gly	Asn	Val	Leu	Val	Thr
Human-Alpha (71–107)	Ala	His	Val	Asp	Asp	Met	Pro	Asn	Ala	Leu	Ser	Ala	Leu	Ser	Asp	Leu	His	Ala	His	Lys	Leu	Arg	Val	Asp	Pro	Val	Asn	Phe	Lys	Leu	Leu	Ser	His	Cys	Leu	Leu	Val
Gorilla-Beta	Ala	His	Leu	Asp	Asn	Leu	Lys	Gly	Thr	Phe	Ala	Thr	Leu	Ser	Glu	Leu	His	Cys	Asp	Lys	Leu	His	Val	Asp	Pro	Glu	Asn	Phe	Lys	Leu	Leu	Gly	Asn	Val	Leu	Val	Cys
Pig-Beta	Lys	His	Leu	Asp	Asn	Leu	Lys	Gly	Thr	Phe	Ala	Lys	Leu	Ser	Glu	Leu	His	Cys	Asp	Glu	Leu	His	Val	Asp	Pro	Glu	Asn	Phe	Arg	Leu	Leu	Gly	Asn	Val	Leu	Val	Cys
Horse-Beta	His	His	Leu	Asp	Asn	Leu	Lys	Gly	Thr	Phe	Ala	Ala	Leu	Ser	Glu	Leu	His	Cys	Asp	Lys	Leu	His	Val	Asp	Pro	Glu	Asn	Phe	Arg	Leu	Leu	Gly	Asn	Val	Leu	Ala	Leu
Whale myoglobin (77–113)	Lys	Lys	Lys	Gly	His	His	Glu	Ala	Glu	Leu	Lys	Pro	Leu	Ala	Gln	Ser	His	Ala	Thr	Lys	His	Lys	Ile	Pro	Ile	Lys	Tyr	Leu	Glu	Phe	Ile	Ser	Glu	Ala	Ile	Ile	His

FIGURE 2.4.

Family resemblances are exhibited by the polypeptide chains found in several kinds of hemoglobin and by the polypeptide chain of sperm-whale myoglobin. Hemoglobin is the oxygen-carrying molecule of the blood; myoglobin stores oxygen in muscle. Polypeptides are molecular chains whose links are amino acid units, usually called residues. The hemoglobin chains comprise either 141 or 146 residues; the myoglobin chain, 153. Each molecule of hemoglobin contains two subunits of a polypeptide chain called alpha (α) and two of a chain called beta (β). In human adults about 2 percent of the hemoglobin molecules contain delta (δ) chains in place of beta chains. Two other chains, gamma (γ) and epsilon (ε, *not shown*), are manufactured during fetal life and can also serve in place of the β-chain. The illustration enables one to compare the four principal chains (α, β, γ, δ) found in human hemoglobin with the β-chains found in the hemoglobin molecules of gorillas, pigs and horses. The δ-, γ- and α-chains are ranked below the human β-chain in order of increasing number of differences. The gorilla β-chain differs from the human β-chain at only one site. The pig β-chain appears to differ at about 17 sites (based on the known differences), and the horse β-chain at 26 sites. The number of differences indicates roughly how far these animals are separated from man on the phylogenetic tree. Relatively few sites have been completely resistant to evolutionary change. Only 11 of the sites (*circles*) have the same residues in all known hemoglobin and myoglobin chains, and only 15 more sites (*triangles*) have the same residues in all known chains of hemoglobin. Among the four principal chains of normal human hemoglobin, the same residues are found at 49 sites. The β-, δ- and γ-chains, which are closely related, have 103 sites in common.

Top block (residues 39–75):

Chain	Sequence
1	Gln(39)-Arg(40)-Phe(41)-Phe(42)-Glu(43)-Ser(44)-Phe(45)-Gly(46)-Asp(47)-Leu(48)-Ser(49)-Thr(50)-Pro(51)-Asp(52)-Ala(53)-Val(54)-Met(55)-Gly(56)-Asn(57)-Pro(58)-Lys(59)-Val(60)-Lys(61)-Ala(62)-His(63)-Gly(64)-Lys(65)-Lys(66)-Val(67)-Leu(68)-Gly(69)-Ala(70)-Phe(71)-Ser(72)-Asp(73)-Gly(74)-Leu(75)
2	Gln(39)-Arg(40)-Phe(41)-Phe(42)-Glu(43)-Ser(44)-Phe(45)-Gly(46)-Asp(47)-Leu(48)-Ser(49)-Ser(50)-Pro(51)-Asp(52)-Ala(53)-Val(54)-Met(55)-Gly(56)-Asn(57)-Pro(58)-Lys(59)-Val(60)-Lys(61)-Ala(62)-His(63)-Gly(64)-Lys(65)-Lys(66)-Val(67)-Leu(68)-Gly(69)-Ala(70)-Phe(71)-Ser(72)-Asp(73)-Gly(74)-Leu(75)
3	Gln(39)-Arg(40)-Phe(41)-Phe(42)-Asp(43)-Ser(44)-Phe(45)-Gly(46)-Asn(47)-Leu(48)-Ser(49)-Ser(50)-Ala(51)-Ser(52)-Ala(53)-Ile(54)-Met(55)-Gly(56)-Asn(57)-Pro(58)-Lys(59)-Val(60)-Lys(61)-Ala(62)-His(63)-Gly(64)-Lys(65)-Lys(66)-Val(67)-Leu(68)-Thr(69)-Ser(70)-Leu(71)-Gly(72)-Asp(73)-Ala(74)-Ile(75)
4	Lys(40)-Thr(41)-Tyr(42)-Phe(43)-Pro(44)-His(45)-Phe(46)- -Asp(47)-Leu(48)-Ser(49)-His(50)-Gly(51)-Ser(52)- - -Ala(53)-Gln(54)-Val(55)-Lys(56)-Gly(57)-His(58)-Gly(59)-Lys(60)-Lys(61)-Val(62)-Ala(63)-Asp(64)-Ala(65)-Leu(66)-Thr(67)-Asn(68)-Ala(69)-Val(70)
5	Gln(39)-Arg(40)-Phe(41)-Phe(42)-Glu(43)-Ser(44)-Phe(45)-Gly(46)-Asp(47)-Leu(48)-Ser(49)-Thr(50)-Pro(51)-Asp(52)-Ala(53)-Val(54)-Met(55)-Gly(56)-Asn(57)-Pro(58)-Lys(59)-Val(60)-Lys(61)-Ala(62)-His(63)-Gly(64)-Lys(65)-Lys(66)-Val(67)-Leu(68)-Gly(69)-Ala(70)-Phe(71)-Ser(72)-Asp(73)-Gly(74)-Leu(75)
6	Gln(39)-Arg(40)-Phe(41)-Phe(42)-Glu(43)-Ser(44)-Phe(45)-Gly(46)-Asp(47)-Leu(48)-Ser(49)-(50)-(51)-Asp(52)-Ala(53)-Val(54)-Met(55)-Gly(56)-Asn(57)-Pro(58)-Lys(59)-Val(60)-Lys(61)-Ala(62)-His(63)-Gly(64)-Lys(65)-Lys(66)-Val(67)-Leu(68)-(69)-(70)-Phe(71)-Ser(72)-Asp(73)-(74)-Leu(75)
7	Gln(39)-Arg(40)-Phe(41)-Phe(42)-Asp(43)-Ser(44)-Phe(45)-Gly(46)-Asp(47)-Leu(48)-Ser(49)-Asp(50)-Pro(51)-Gly(52)-Ala(53)-Val(54)-Met(55)-Gly(56)-Asn(57)-Pro(58)-Lys(59)-Val(60)-Lys(61)-Ala(62)-His(63)-Gly(64)-Lys(65)-Lys(66)-Val(67)-Leu(68)-His(69)-Ser(70)-Phe(71)-Gly(72)-Glu(73)-Gly(74)-Val(75)
8	Leu(40)-Glu(41)-Lys(42)-Phe(43)-Asp(44)-Arg(45)-Phe(46)-Lys(47)-His(48)-Leu(49)-Lys(50)-Thr(51)-Glu(52)-Ala(53)-Glu(54)-Met(55)-Lys(56)-Ala(57)-Ser(58)-Glu(59)-Asp(60)-Leu(61)-Lys(62)-Lys(63)-His(64)-Gly(65)-Val(66)-Thr(67)-Val(68)-Leu(69)-Thr(70)-Ala(71)-Leu(72)-Gly(73)-Ala(74)-Ile(75)-Leu(76)

Bottom block (residues 116–153):

1	His(116)-His(117)-Phe(118)-Gly(119)-Lys(120)-Glu(121)-Phe(122)-Thr(123)-Pro(124)-Pro(125)-Val(126)-Gln(127)-Ala(128)-Ala(129)-Tyr(130)-Gln(131)-Lys(132)-Val(133)-Val(134)-Ala(135)-Gly(136)-Val(137)-Ala(138)-Asn(139)-Ala(140)-Leu(141)-Ala(142)-His(143)-Lys(144)-Tyr(145)-His(146)	Human-Beta
2	Arg(116)-Asn(117)-Phe(118)-Gly(119)-Lys(120)-Glu(121)-Phe(122)-Thr(123)-Pro(124)-Gln(125)-Met(126)-Gln(127)-Ala(128)-Ala(129)-Tyr(130)-Gln(131)-Lys(132)-Val(133)-Val(134)-Ala(135)-Gly(136)-Val(137)-Ala(138)-Asn(139)-Ala(140)-Leu(141)-Ala(142)-His(143)-Lys(144)-Tyr(145)-His(146)	Human-Delta
3	Ile(116)-His(117)-Phe(118)-Gly(119)-Lys(120)-Glu(121)-Phe(122)-Thr(123)-Pro(124)-Glu(125)-Val(126)-Gln(127)-Ala(128)-Ser(129)-Trp(130)-Gln(131)-Lys(132)-Met(133)-Val(134)-Thr(135)-Gly(136)-Val(137)-Ala(138)-Ser(139)-Ala(140)-Leu(141)-Ser(142)-Ser(143)-Arg(144)-Tyr(145)-His(146)	Human-Gamma
4	Ala(111)-His(112)-Leu(113)-Pro(114)-Ala(115)-Glu(116)-Phe(117)-Thr(118)-Pro(119)-Ala(120)-Val(121)-His(122)-Ala(123)-Ser(124)-Leu(125)-Asp(126)-Lys(127)-Phe(128)-Leu(129)-Ala(130)-Ser(131)-Val(132)-Ser(133)-Thr(134)-Val(135)-Leu(136)-Thr(137)-Ser(138)-Lys(139)-Tyr(140)-Arg(141)	Human-Alpha
5	His(116)-His(117)-Phe(118)-Gly(119)-Lys(120)-Glu(121)-Phe(122)-Thr(123)-Pro(124)-Pro(125)-Val(126)-Gln(127)-Ala(128)-Ala(129)-Tyr(130)-Gln(131)-Lys(132)-Val(133)-Val(134)-Ala(135)-Gly(136)-Val(137)-Ala(138)-Asn(139)-Ala(140)-Leu(141)-Ala(142)-His(143)-Lys(144)-Tyr(145)-His(146)	Gorilla-Beta
6	Arg(116)-Arg(117)-Phe(118)-Gly(119)-(120)-(121)-(122)-(123)-(124)-(125)-(126)-(127)-(128)-(129)-(130)-(131)-Lys(132)-Val(133)-Val(134)-Ala(135)-Gly(136)-Val(137)-Ala(138)-Ala(139)-Ala(140)-Leu(141)-Ala(142)-His(143)-Lys(144)-Tyr(145)-His(146)	Pig-Beta
7	Arg(116)-His(117)-Phe(118)-Gly(119)-Lys(120)-Asp(121)-Phe(122)-Thr(123)-Pro(124)-Glu(125)-Leu(126)-Gln(127)-Ala(128)-Ser(129)-Tyr(130)-Gln(131)-Lys(132)-Val(133)-Val(134)-Ala(135)-Gly(136)-Val(137)-Ala(138)-Asn(139)-Ala(140)-Leu(141)-Ala(142)-His(143)-Lys(144)-Tyr(145)-His(146)	Horse-Beta
8	Ser(117)-Arg(118)-His(119)-Pro(120)-Gly(121)-Asn(122)-Phe(123)-Gly(124)-Ala(125)-Asp(126)-Ala(127)-Gln(128)-Gly(129)-Ala(130)-Met(131)-Asn(132)-Lys(133)-Ala(134)-Leu(135)-Glu(136)-Leu(137)-Phe(138)-Arg(139)-Lys(140)-Asp(141)-Ile(142)- -Ala(144)-Lys(145)-Tyr(146)-Lys(147)-Glu(148)-Leu(149)-Gly(150)-Tyr(151)-Gln(152)-Gly(153)	Whale myoglobin

Hemoglobin chains (bracket grouping Human-Beta, Human-Delta, Human-Gamma, Human-Alpha, Gorilla-Beta, Pig-Beta, Horse-Beta)

Amino acid abbreviations:

ALA	ALANINE	**GLN**	GLUTAMINE	**LEU**	LEUCINE	**SER**	SERINE
ARG	ARGININE	**GLU**	GLUTAMIC ACID	**LYS**	LYSINE	**THR**	THREONINE
ASN	ASPARAGINE	**GLY**	GLYCINE	**MET**	METHIONINE	**TRP**	TRYPTOPHAN
ASP	ASPARTIC ACID	**HIS**	HISTIDINE	**PHE**	PHENYLALANINE	**TYR**	TYROSINE
CYS	CYSTEINE	**ILE**	ISOLEUCINE	**PRO**	PROLINE	**VAL**	VALINE

Legend:

- RESIDUE THE SAME IN ALL CHAINS SHOWN
- ● RESIDUE THE SAME IN ALL KNOWN HEMOGLOBIN AND MYOGLOBIN CHAINS
- RESIDUE THE SAME IN ALL HEMOGLOBIN CHAINS SHOWN
- ▲ RESIDUE THE SAME IN ALL KNOWN HEMOGLOBIN CHAINS
- RESIDUE THE SAME IN FOUR MAIN HUMAN HEMOGLOBIN CHAINS
- RESIDUE THE SAME AS THAT IN HUMAN BETA CHAIN
- RESIDUE DIFFERENT FROM THAT IN HUMAN BETA CHAIN
- RESIDUE NOT DETERMINED

(SOME RESIDUE ASSIGNMENTS ARE TENTATIVE)

3. Three-Dimensional Folding of a Polypeptide

Using short lengths of coated wire, fold two alpha (white) and two beta (black) chains of hemoglobin as shown in Figures 2.5-2.12. The chain-folding pattern is actually that of myoglobin, but it is quite similar to that of hemoglobin (see Figure 2.4).

a. Take the wire, leave ½ inch straight, and take four turns around a pencil (see Figure 2.5). If you hold the point toward you, the turns must go clockwise away from you to be an alpha helix. Otherwise you will get a beta helix, which is not found in nature (see Figure 2.2).

b. Leaving 1 inch straight, take another four turns for the B region, then leave another ½ inch straight, and take two turns for the C region (see Figure 2.6).

c. Now slide the pencil out until the point is in the C helix region (see Figure 2.7). Leaving 2 inches straight, take one turn (D helix); leave ½ inch straight and take four turns (E helix); leave 1½ inches straight, and take two turns for the F region.

d. Slide the pencil down so the point is in the F helix region, leave 1 inch straight, and take five turns for the G region.

e. Slide the pencil out until the point is in the G region, leave ¾ inch straight, and take six turns for the H region. You now have a polypeptide chain with eight helical regions interspersed with random coil regions of appropriate lengths.

f. Lay the chain on the desk so that the straight portions (random coils) are down. Then, using a fingernail as a fulcrum, press against the center of the first one inch of straight wire and bend coil A upward at a 90-degree angle.

g. Pick up the chain and orient it above Figure 2-8 so that coils A and B of the chain and the diagram correspond. They will lay in the front face of the cube, and the apex of the first V angle you bent will point to your left.

h. Now bend the half-inch straight portion between coils B and C closely behind B, so that the remainder of the chain points toward the back lower edge of the cube (Figure 2-9).

i. Bend the two-inch random wire between coils C and D closely behind C, so that the remainder returns to the front, leaving coil C at the center of the floor of the cube as the apex of a second V angle that is perpendicular to the first one, and leaving coil D forward and in the front right bottom corner of the cube in the same plate as A and B (Figure 2-9).

j. Then bend the one-half inch between coils D and E closely behind D upward at 90 degrees (Figure 2-10).

k. Curve the middle of the two-inch stretch between E and F into a 180-degree turn downward, so that F stands directly behind E and the third V angle has been formed (Figure 2-10).

l. Bend the middle of the 1½-inch stretch at 90 degrees, so that the remainder points to the left, and G is behind the plane of A and B in the center of the cube (Figure 2-11).

m. Bend the last straight section 180 degrees, so that H moves in behind G in the center of the back face of the cube to form the fourth V angle (Figure 2-11).

n. The heme group is held in a partially exposed pocket from the random region between F and G (Figure 2-12).

o. Check the chain against the display model.

p. Repeat steps *a* through *o* three more times.

q. Using fine wire, hang the four chains from a ring stand to give the complete quarternary structure of hemoglobin. You are welcome to take the polypeptide chains home for future reference and for decoration.

FIGURE 2.5.
Helical regions of hemoglobin model.

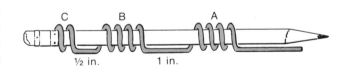

FIGURE 2.6.
Helical regions of hemoglobin model.

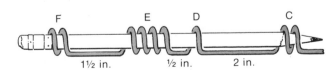

FIGURE 2.7.
Helical regions of hemoglobin model.

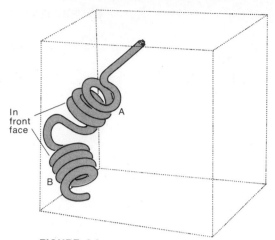

FIGURE 2.8.

Three-dimensional folding of hemoglobin model.

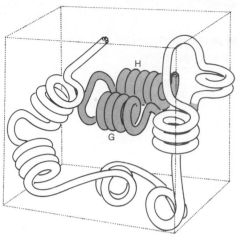

FIGURE 2.11.

Over-all view of hemoglobin subunit model.

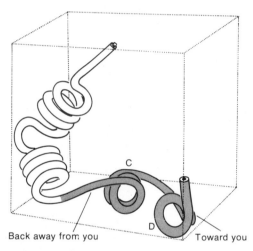

FIGURE 2.9.

Three-dimensional folding of hemoglobin model.

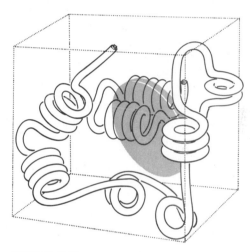

FIGURE 2.12.

Position of heme group in model.

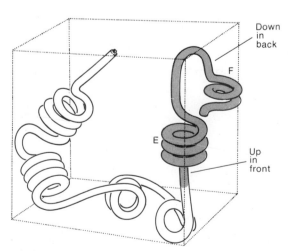

FIGURE 2.10.

Three-dimensional folding of hemoglobin model.

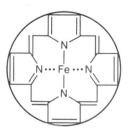

FIGURE 2.13.

Model of heme prosthetic group.

FIGURE 2.14.

Sequence of amino acid units in the model of myoglobin is indicated by the letters and numbers in the illustration. The amino acid unit represented by each symbol is given in the table; the key to the abbreviations is at top left in the table. The brackets in the table indicate those amino acid units that form a helical section. The direction of the main chain is traced in black and gray in the illustration; the chain begins at far left (*amino end*) and ends near the top (*carboxyl end*). The heme group is indicated by the outlined gray surrounding the sphere. Not all the amino acid units in the model have been positively identified. For some it has only been determined that they cannot be certain units. The over-all configuration of the molecule, however, is known with considerable confidence.

ALANINE ALA	C- 1 HIS	FG- 1 (NOT GLY)
ARGININE ARG	2 PRO	2 (NOT GLY)
ASPARTIC ACID ASP	3 GLU	3 PHE
ASPARAGINE ASN	4 THR	4 (NOT ALA)
GLUTAMIC ACID GLN	5 LEU	5 ILEU
OR GLUTAMINE	6 GLU	G- 1 PRO
GLUTAMIC ACID GLU	7 LYS	2 ILEU
GLYCINE GLY	CD- 1 PHE	3 LYS
HISTIDINE HIS	2 ASP	4 TYR
ISOLEUCENE ILE	3 ARG	5 (NOT ALA, GLY)
LEUCINE LEU	4 PHE	6 GLU
LYSINE LYS	5 LYS	7 HIS
METHIONINE MET	6 HIS	8 LEU
PHENYLALANINE PHE	2 GLU	9 SER
PROLINE PRO	3 ALA	10 (NOT GLY, ALA)
SERINE SER	D- 7 LEU	11 ALA
THREONINE THR	8 LYS	12 VAL OR THR
TYROSINE TYR	1 THR	13 ILEU
VALINE VAL	4 GLU	14 HIS
	5 MET	15 VAL
	6 LYS	16 ARG
	7 ALA	17 ALA
	E- 1 SER	18 THR
	2 GLU	19 LYS
A- 1 VAL (AMINO END)	3 ASP	GH- 1 HIS
2 ALA	4 LEU	2 ASP
3 GLY	5 LYS	3 ASP
4 GLU	6 VAL	4 GLU
5 TYR	7 HIS	5 PHE
6 SER	8 GLY	6 GLY
7 GLU	9 ILEU	H- 1 ALA
8 ILEU	10 GLU	2 PRO
9 LEU	11 VAL	3 ALA
10 LYS	12 ASP	4 ASP
11 (NOT GLY)	13 (NOT ALA, GLY)	5 GLY
12 TYR	14 ALA	6 ALA
13 (NOT GLY)	15 LEU	7 MET
14 LEU	16 GLY	8 GLY
15 LEU	17 ALA	9 LYS
16 GLU	18 ILEU	10 ALA
AB- 1 (NOT GLY)	19 ASP	11 LEU
B- 1 LEU	20 ARG	12 GLU
2 VAL OR THR	EF- 1 LYS	13 LEU
3 ALA	2 LYS	14 PHE
4 GLY	3 GLY	15 ARG
5 HIS	4 LEU	16 LYS
6 GLY	5 HIS	17 ASP
7 LYS	6 (NOT GLY)	18 ILEU
8 LEU	7 (NOT GLY)	19 ALA
9 THR	8 GLU	20 ALA
10 LEU	F- 1 GLU	21 LYS
11 ILEU	2 ALA	22 TYR
12 SER	3 PRO	23 LYS
13 LEU	4 THR	24 GLU
14 PHE	5 ALA	HC- 1 LEU
15 LYS	6 HIS	2 GLY
16 SER	7 SER	3 TYR
	8 HIS	4 GLY
	9 ALA	5 GLU (CARBOXYL END)

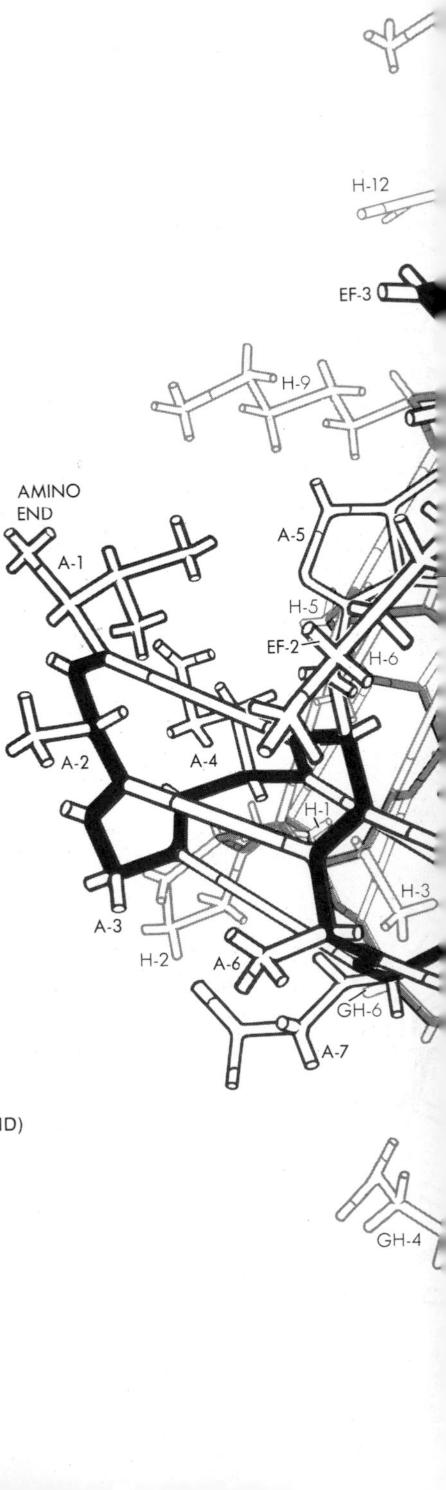

(From J. C. Kendrew, "The Three-dimensional Structure of a Protein Molecule."

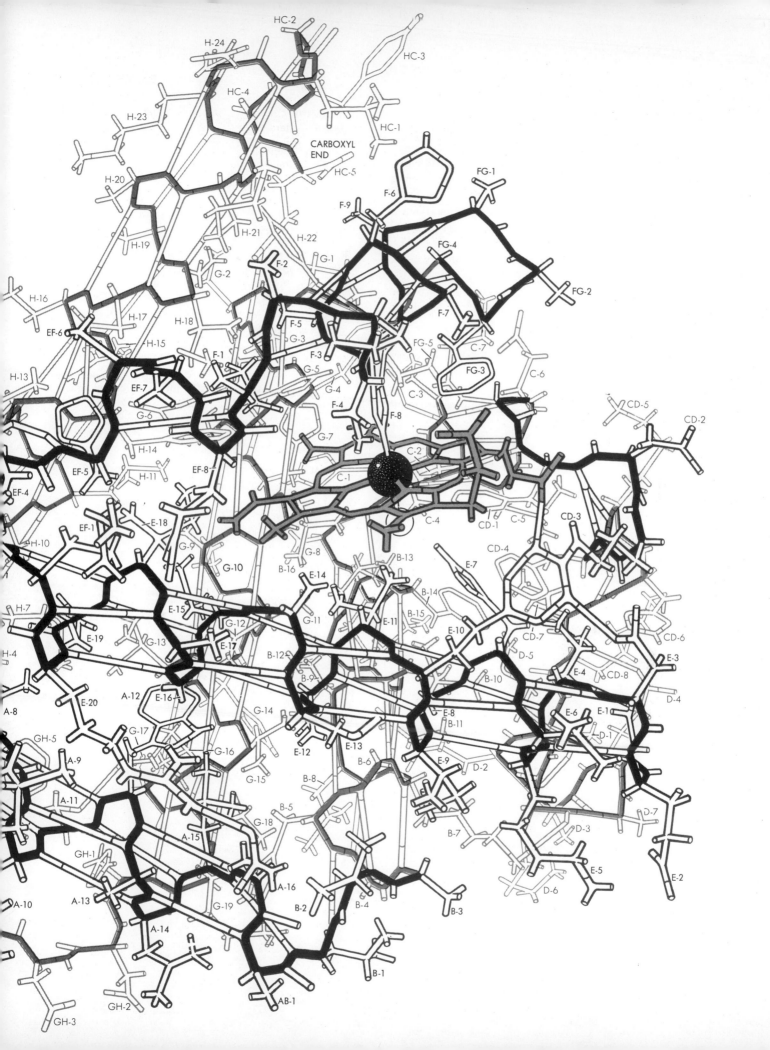

NOTES AND REVIEW QUESTIONS

1. Why can't you have D- and L-isomers of glycine?
2. You wish to prepare a synthetic soy sauce like that used in Chinese restaurants. You will make it up as a mixture of commercially available synthetic chemicals. You know the main flavor ingredient is glutamic acid, and that real soy sauce is prepared from the fermentation of soybeans. How do you suppose using D-glutamic acid would affect the quality of your product? Why?
3. Referring to the sketches you have made of D- and L-alanine, draw the D- and L-isomers of serine.
4. When you turned all the helices in the wire, what level of protein structure had you partly described?
5. When you bent the helices into their proper orientation, what level of protein structure were you describing?
6. When you assembled the four chains on the ring stand, what level of protein structure were you describing?
7. What is the prosthetic group of hemoglobin?

REFERENCES

1. R. E. Dickerson and I. Geis, *The Structure and Action of Proteins* (Harper & Row, 1969).
2. P. Doty, "Proteins," *Scientific American*, September 1957. Offprint No. 7.
3. R. V. Eck and M. O. Dayhoff, *Atlas of Protein Sequence and Structure* (National Biomedical Research Foundation, 1969).
4. M. F. Perutz, "The Hemoglobin Molecule," *Scientific American*, November 1964. Offprint No. 196.
5. E. Zuckerkandl, "The Evolution of Hemoglobin," *Scientific American*, May 1965. Offprint No. 1012.

THE CARE AND HANDLING OF PROTEINS

Size, Measurement of Concentration, Enzymatic Splitting of Proteins, and Separating Mixtures of Proteins

The four parts of this experiment illustrate some of the central phenomena of protein chemistry. Before one can begin any intelligent study of the structure or function of a protein, one must be able to purify it. Selective precipitation with ammonium sulfate and column chromatography are among the most useful methods for purifying proteins. Dialysis, used here to indicate the difference in size between the molecules of proteins and of simple inorganic salts, is also commonly used in the laboratory to purify proteins. In any attempt to study proteins, one must be able to measure the amount of protein in a sample. The Biuret test is a quantitative assay of protein concentration. Proteolytic enzymes split proteins into small fragments; their activity, which must be guarded against in the isolation of certain proteins, has been put to good use in determining the amino acid sequence of some proteins and in making stain removers and meat tenderizers. Several methods for the measurement of protease activity are illustrated.

EXPERIMENTAL PROCEDURES

1. Dialysis

It is frequently necessary to separate proteins from small molecules such as salts, and this is easily done by dialysis. The salt-protein mixture is placed in a sack of membrane such as sausage casing is made from. The membrane has pores large enough to let water and small molecules pass through, but too small to allow the passage of protein. You will be given two test tubes—one contains a yellow inorganic salt (potassium ferricyanide), and the other a chromoprotein (hemoglobin or phycocyanin). Mix the two together, and note the color. Take a length of dialysis tubing that has been left soaking in water to make it soft and pliable, and tie two knots close together at one end. Put 4 or 5 ml of your ferricyanide-chromoprotein mixture in this sack with an eyedropper, and tie off the open end. Label the sack with a small string tag so you will be able to identify it. Place it in the large vat of stirred water, and leave it till the end of the period. Then empty the contents into a test tube by piercing the sack, and observe the color. Also note the color of the water in the stirred vat before and after the experiment.

2. Protein Standard Curve

It is frequently necessary to measure the amount of protein present in a solution, and this is conveniently done by the Biuret reaction. Alkaline copper sulfate turns various shades of blue when mixed with protein. The color achieved with an unknown sample is compared with those of a series of standard solutions containing known amounts of protein. This experiment is simply meant to show that the intensity of the blue color is proportional to the amount of protein present. Take five numbered tubes, and add 0.0, 0.5, 1.0, 1.5, and 2.0 ml of the solution of standard protein (10 mg/ml) from the burette. In another tube, add 2.0 ml of casein hydrolysate (10 mg/ml). Add water from a burette so that all the tubes contain a liquid volume of 2.0 ml. Now add 8 ml of Biuret reagent from a burette to each tube, and let them stand for 30 minutes. Judge the relative color intensities by eye: record them. Now measure the color intensities—i.e., absorbances—in the colorimeter, and record the numerical values. (Your instructor will give detailed instructions on the use of a colorimeter.) Later make a graph, plotting absorbance values (on the vertical axis) against the amount of protein added (on the horizontal axis).

3. Enzyme-Catalyzed Breakdown of Proteins

Proteases are proteins that catalyze the splitting—hydrolysis, addition of water across peptide bonds—of proteins (see Figure 3.1).

a. A qualitative demonstration of the action of a protease in destroying a protein structure is done as follows. Take two small gelatin capsules (such as can be purchased at the local drugstore) and carefully open them. Add 1 or 2 drops of blue dye (to make the results more obvious) to the larger half of each. Fill one capsule with water, and fill the other with the trypsin (a common protease) solution provided. Close the capsules and drop them into separate 25-ml beakers of water. Label the beakers so you can tell which is which. Observe what has happened at the end of the period, and record it.

b. Protease activity is measured quantitatively by observing the amount of color produced when, for example, a nearly colorless compound, para-nitrophenyl acetate, is hydrolyzed by proteases to give the intensely yellow nitrophenol. Alternatively, insoluble proteins of leather may be chemically reacted with a blue dye to give a water-insoluble blue leather powder. When a protease attacks this substrate, small pieces of protein, with dye attached, are broken off and dissolve in the water; the blue color of the solution is a measure of the protease activity.

Each student will be provided with three tubes, labeled S, that contain the substrate and buffer, and with three tubes, labeled B, that contain only buffer and that will be used as enzyme blanks. Separate the tubes into three pairs, each pair containing one S and one B tube. To each of the first pair, add 1 ml (0.2 mg) of trypsin. To each of the second pair, add 1 ml (6.0 mg) of Axion—a clotheswashing product advertised as containing enzymes. To each of the third pair, add 1 ml of solution of Adolph's meat tenderizer (6.0 mg). Label the pairs of tubes carefully so that you can distinguish them. Take a seventh tube containing substrate only. Add 1 ml of buffer to this tube, and label it SB for "substrate blank." Allow these solutions to stand for 30 to 45 minutes. Be sure to record the duration of this incubation period; you will need it later. Using a water blank, set the colorimeter for 100% transmittance at the proper wavelength (400 nm for the para-nitrophenyl acetate assay, 625 for the hide-azure blue assay). Read and record the absorbances of the substrate blank, the three enzyme blanks, and the three complete-reaction mixtures.

4. Protein Separation

Protein fractionation is where most biochemistry begins, since one must frequently purify one specific protein from the thousands of kinds of proteins found in any tissue. The various proteins may be sorted out in terms of their different solubilities in varying concentrations of salt, their varying molecular sizes, and their varying ionic charges. You will use mixtures of visibly colored proteins to simplify observation of their separation. However, since most proteins have no visible color, you must use other specific criteria to recognize them.

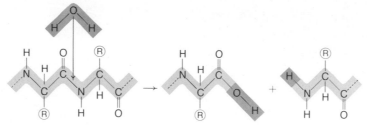

FIGURE 3.1.

Cleavage of a "peptide" bond is the fundamental step in the degradation, or digestion, of a protein molecule. A peptide bond is the carbon-nitrogen linkage formed when two amino acids are united, with the simultaneous release of a molecule of water. The reverse process, peptide hydrolysis, is shown here. Without a catalyst, hydrolysis is immeasurably slow. The letter "R" represents any of the various side groups found in the 20 common amino acids from which the polypeptide chains of proteins are assembled. (From H. Neurath, "Protein-digesting Enzymes." Copyright © 1964 by Scientific American, Inc. All rights reserved.)

a. Ammonium sulfate is used for selective precipitation of proteins, since: it will form salts with some of the ionized sidechains, decreasing the solubility of some proteins; it will form bridged salts between some proteins, causing them to precipitate; and it will gradually remove water from around the proteins as the salt binds up the water of hydration.

Take 4 ml of a crude extract of blue-green algae in a centrifuge tube. These plants contain the green chlorophyll protein complex, the blue protein phycocyanin, several yellow and red proteins, and several thousand kinds of colorless proteins. Add 1 ml of saturated ammonium sulfate solution and mix. This will give a concentration of ammonium sulfate that is 20 per cent of saturation. Let it stand 10 minutes, then centrifuge it, using a balance tube. Observe the color of the precipitate. Pour off the supernatant solution into another tube, and mix it with an additional 5 ml of saturated ammonium sulfate solution to give 60 per cent of saturation. Let it stand 10 minutes, then centrifuge it, using a balance tube. Observe and record the colors of the precipitate and the supernatant liquid.

b. Gel filtration is used to sort proteins according to their size. The gel particles are like bowling balls with many finger holes all over them (see Figure 3.2). Small molecules can enter the holes but big molecules cannot; so the big molecules can only flow past the balls and run quickly through the gel column, while small molecules wander into the holes and are delayed in their passage through the column. Large aggregates of molecules cannot even penetrate the spaces between the balls; so they remain at the top of the gel column. One can obtain various types of gels with varying hole sizes to separate various kinds of molecules.

Each student will be given a small column of Sephadex G-100 gel. When you are ready to start the separation, call the instructor and he will carefully put a few drops of a protein mixture (phycocyanin and cytochrome c, or hemoglobin and cytochrome c) on the column. Allow this to enter the gel completely, then add water carefully with the dropper provided. Don't let the column run dry—always keep a small reservoir of water on top. When one of the proteins has nearly reached the bottom, stopper the column so that no more liquid flows through. Make a sketch of the column indicating the colors of the bands.

c. Ion-exchange chromatography is used to sort proteins in terms of the relative strength of the ionic bonding between ionically charged groups on the proteins and ionically charged groups that are permanently built onto insoluble cellulose particles. Varying concentrations of salt are then used to displace the protein, the salt taking the place of the protein at the charged sites on the column. Proteins with the same charge sign (+ or −) as the column material do not bind and simply pass through. If the protein has a weak charge, opposite in sign to that of the column, it will bind but can be displaced by a dilute salt solution. If the protein is highly charged and opposite in sign to the charge on the column, only a strong salt solution will displace it.

Each student will be given a small column filled with DEAE cellulose (anion exchange). When you are ready, the instructor will put a small

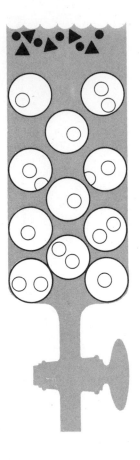

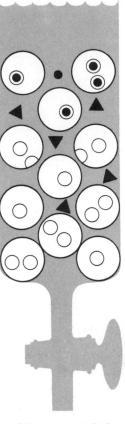

Little ones penetrate
pores in the beads.

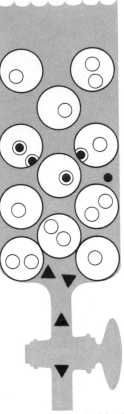

Little ones are retarded in their
passage, since they keep
blundering into pores.

FIGURE 3.2.
Gel-filtration chromatography.

amount of protein mixture (algal protein, which is mainly phycocyanin and cytochrome c) on the column. Wash the column successively with 3 ml each of H_2O, 0.1N NaCl, 0.2N NaCl, 0.3N NaCl, and 0.5N NaCl, collecting each eluate in a separate tube. Observe and record the migration of variously colored materials through the column in relation to the salt concentration used. Don't let the column run dry at any stage.

NOTES AND REVIEW QUESTIONS

1. Write a one-page summary of what you have done in this lab and why.
2. What happened to the solution you dialyzed? Why do you stir the water in the dialysis bath? Some types of kidney disease can only be treated by re-

moving low-molecular-weight, toxic substances from the patient's blood. How might this be done?
3. Trypsin alters the gelatin capsule in a way that tells you what gelatin is. Here you are using a pure enzyme of known specificity to identify the substrate. What kind of substrate molecules is the gelatin capsule made of? What normally releases the medicine from gelatin capsules when you swallow them?
4. Tabulate your data from the measurement of protease activity with the artificial substrate. Reason out which blank values should be subtracted from the readings of the complete reaction mixture to give an accurate estimate of substrate splitting. The potency of an enzyme preparation is usually called the *specific activity,* and is quantitatively described by the measured change of substrate per unit time per unit weight of enzyme. Calculate the specific activities of the three enzyme preparations used in

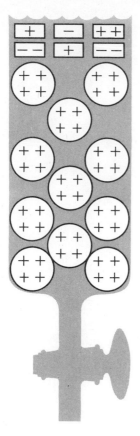
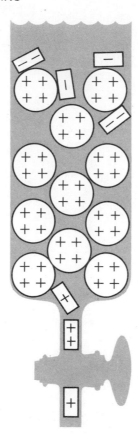
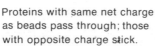
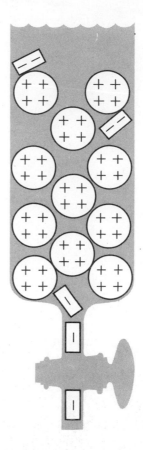

Proteins with same net charge
as beads pass through; those
with opposite charge stick.

Weak salt solution displaces
weakly held protein.

FIGURE 3.3.
Ion-exchange chromatography.

part 3b, as change in absorbance per minute per mg of protein. Would you wash a wool sweater in Axion? How does Adolph's meat tenderizer work?

4. Look at your sketch of the Sephadex column experiment from part 4b. Were the proteins separated? Which protein had the higher molecular weight?

5. Explain briefly what happened when you added successive salt solutions to the DEAE column. What are the relative strengths of binding of the visibly colored proteins to DEAE? Are the visibly colored proteins simple or conjugated proteins?

REFERENCES

1. A. A. Green and W. L. Hughes, "Protein Fractionation on the Basis of Solubility in Aqueous Solutions of Salts and Organic Solvents," in S. P. Colowick and N. O. Kaplan, eds., *Methods in Enzymology* (Academic Press, 1955), I, 67.

2. H. Neurath, "Protein-Digesting Enzymes," *Scientific American,* December 1964. Offprint No. 198.

3. E. A. Peterson and H. A. Sober, "Column Chromatography of Proteins: Substituted Celluloses," in Colowick and Kaplan, eds., *Methods in Enzymology* (Academic Press, 1962), V, 3.

AN ENZYME, INORGANIC PYROPHOSPHATASE

the General Phenomena of Enzyme Catalysis

In this experiment you will use an enzyme, inorganic pyrophosphatase, to illustrate the general characteristics of enzyme activity described in your text. This enzyme is found in all tissues, and plays an important role in the energy metabolism of the cell. It is relatively stable, highly active, and easy to measure. You will use a crude tissue extract as a source of enzyme activity rather than a purified protein, but, in the light of the previous experiments, you can readily see how you might purify this enzyme, possibly to the point where all other kinds of proteins were eliminated from your preparation.

Inorganic pyrophosphatase is easily obtained by breaking open the cells of almost any tissue. Since this enzyme is soluble, that is, not permanently attached to any of the subcellular structures, an easy first step in purification is to filter out the particulate matter. Having the soluble tissue extract, one must be able to measure the activity of the enzyme; this is conveniently done by measuring the amount of inorganic phosphate that is produced in the enzymatic hydrolysis of inorganic pyrophosphate (see Figure 4.1). Inorganic phosphate can be made to react with suit-able reagents—suitable because they do not react with pyrophosphate—to give a blue color, the intensity of which is proportional to the amount of phosphate present. You will prepare a phosphate standard curve, relating known amounts of inorganic phosphate to the measurable blue color produced in the assay procedure. With this quantitative and specific measurement of product formation, one can test the tissue extract for pyrophosphate-splitting activity. The enzyme ac-

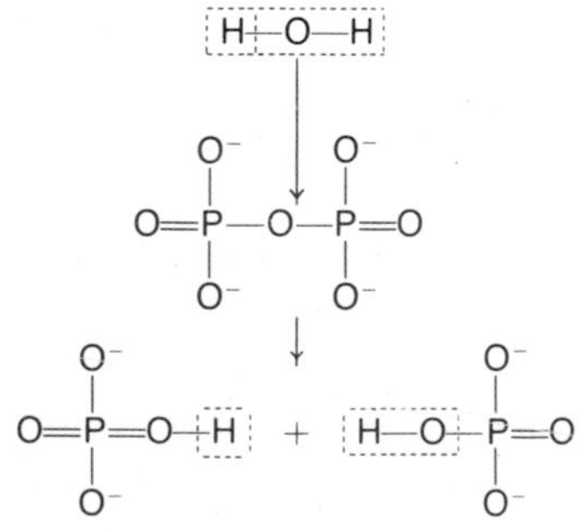

FIGURE 4.1.

Hydrolysis of inorganic pyrophosphate.

tivity is then compared to the chemical hydrolysis of pyrophosphate, which requires cooking this substrate in strong acid. The living cell was obliged to invent the more gentle enzymatic splitting, since it could not contain a strong acid. Next you are to characterize the enzyme in terms of how variations in enzyme concentration, pH, temperature, and metal-ion concentration affect its activity. These are fundamental operations that you will use to characterize any enzyme you might deal with in the course of your career.

EXPERIMENTAL PROCEDURES

1. Phosphate Standard Curve

Inorganic pyrophosphatase catalyzes the cleavage of $P_2O_7^{-4}$ to HPO_4^{-2}. The amount of enzyme present is determined by measuring the amount of HPO_4^{-2} produced from $P_2O_4^{-7}$ in some unit of time, and then by computing the specific activity in terms of micromoles of HPO_4^{-2} produced per minute per ml of crude tissue extract. The amount of HPO_4^{-2} produced is measured in the colorimeter. In practice, this is accomplished by adding $P_2O_7^{-4}$ and enzyme to a test tube, waiting for two minutes to allow the enzyme to catalyze some hydrolysis of the substrate, and then adding the stopping reagent. This reagent contains the acid molybdate to form the blue color, and in addition is acid enough to destroy the enzyme and stop the reaction.

In order to measure the extent of reaction, you must make a standard curve, so that the amount of blue color can be translated into the amount of phosphate produced.

Place six tubes in a rack and make additions to them as shown in Table 4.1. Now add 2.5 ml of the

TABLE 4.1.

Concentrations for a Phosphate Standard Curve.

Add	Tube No.					
	1	2	3	4	5	6
H_2O	1.0[a]	0.8	0.6	0.4	0.2	—
Phosphate standard, 1 μmole per ml	—	0.2	0.4	0.6	0.8	1.0

[a]Units are ml.

stopping reagent to each tube from your burette. Wait ten minutes for color development, and measure the intensity of color development in the colorimeter at 620 nm. Record all the values from the absorbance or optical density scale.

Prepare a standard curve by plotting on graph paper the absorbance on the vertical axis and the μmoles of phosphate added on the horizontal axis. The standard phosphate solution was made by carefully weighing an amount of pure inorganic phosphate and dissolving it in distilled water of measured volume to give one micromole (μmole) of phosphate per ml.

2. Enzyme Extraction and Measurement

You will be given a gram of cut maize leaf. Place this in a chilled mortar with 20 ml of cold 0.1M Tris-HCl buffer, pH 8.5. Add about one spoonful of sand, and grind it until there are no pieces larger than the word "word" printed on this page. Filter this mixture into a beaker through Whatman No. 1 filter paper until you have collected at least 12 ml of extract. Keep this extract on ice.

Now you must determine how much enzyme activity is present in the extract, since the amount of activity present depends on the health of the leaf and on how thoroughly you ground the leaf sample. A summary of the reaction mixtures you will prepare is given in the Table 4.2.

TABLE 4.2.

Measurement of Enzyme Activity.

Add	Tube No.				
	1	2	3	4	5
Substrate (No. 1)	0.6[a]	0.6	0.6	—	0.6
$MgCl_2$ (A)	0.2	0.2	0.2	—	0.2
Tris buffer	—	0.18	0.196	0.8	0.2
Enzyme extract	0.2	0.02	0.004	0.2	—
Stopping reagent	2.5	2.5	2.5	2.5	2.5

[a]Units are ml.

To begin, you must prepare two dilutions of your extract. For the 1-in-10 dilution, add 9 ml of Tris buffer to 1 ml of your extract. For the 1-in-50 dilution, add 9.8 ml of Tris buffer to 0.2 ml of your extract.

Take 3 test tubes, and number them 1, 2, and 3. In each, place 0.6 ml of pyrophosphate substrate Stock Solution No. 1 and 0.2 ml of $MgCl_2$ Stock Solution A. In Tube 1, place 0.2 ml of your undiluted extract. In Tube 2, place 0.2 ml of your 1-in-10 dilution. In Tube 3, place 0.2 ml of your 1-in-50 dilution. Wait two minutes, add 2.5 ml of the stopping reagent to each tube, and shake each one. Set these three tubes aside to incubate for ten minutes.

To get an accurate measurement of the activity of the enzyme, you must know how much inorganic phosphate there is in your enzyme extract. Take another test tube, number it 4, and in it place 0.2 ml of your undiluted extract, 0.8 ml of Tris buffer, and 2.5 ml of the stopping reagent. Shake the tube, and set it aside to incubate for ten minutes also.

To get an accurate measurement, you must also know where the "zero" is on the scale you are using, and must therefore prepare an enzyme blank. Take a fifth test tube, number it 5, and in it place 0.6 ml of Stock Solution No. 1, 0.2 ml of Stock Solution A, 0.2 ml of Tris buffer, and 2.5 ml of the stopping reagent. Use this tube to set the colorimeter to zero at 620 nm.

At the end of the ten-minute incubation period, read the first four tubes in the colorimeter at 620 nm; record the readings, and from them calculate a dilution of your extract that will give you a reasonable change in absorbance (between 0.2 and 0.3) in the two-minute incubation. Dilute the remainder of your extract by this calculated amount for use in the subsequent parts of this experiment.

3. Chemical Hydrolysis of Pyrophosphate

To two test tubes, add 0.1 ml of pyrophosphate Stock Solution No. 2, and 0.4 ml of HCl (1.25N, from a burette; *do not pipette*). Place a marble over one of these tubes and put it in a boiling water bath for 7 minutes. Then to each tube add 0.5 ml of 1N NaOH (from a burette; *do not pipette*), and 2.5 ml of stopping reagent; wait 10 minutes, and read at 620 nm.

4. Reaction Velocity as a Function of Enzyme Concentration

Make additions to 4 tubes as shown in Table 4.3.

TABLE 4.3.

Reaction Velocity and Enzyme Concentration.

Add	Tube No.			
	1	2	3	4
Substrate (No. 2)	0.3[a]	0.3	0.3	0.3
MgCl$_2$ (A)	0.2	0.2	0.2	0.2
Tris buffer, pH 8.5	0.4	0.3	0.1	—
Enzyme	0.1	0.2	0.4	0.5

[a] Units are ml.

After adding the enzyme, wait two minutes for each tube, then add 2.5 ml of the stopping reagent. Wait 10 minutes, then read and record the absorbance at 620 nm.

5. Reaction Velocity as a Function of pH

Make additions to three test tubes as shown in Table 4.4. After adding the enzyme, wait exactly two min-

TABLE 4.4.

Reaction Velocity and pH.

Add	Tube No.		
	1	2	3
Substrate (No. 1) buffered to pH 8.5	0.6[a]	—	—
Substrate (No. 3) buffered to pH 5.0	—	0.6	—
Substrate (No. 4) buffered to pH 11.0	—	—	0.6
MgCl$_2$ (A)	0.2	0.2	0.2
Enzyme	0.2	0.2	0.2

[a] Units are ml.

utes for each tube before adding 2.5 ml of the stopping reagent. Allow the color to develop for 10 minutes, then read and record the absorbance.

6. Enzyme Activity as a Function of Temperature

Add 0.6 ml of substrate (No. 1) and 0.2 ml of MgCl$_2$ (A) to each of four test tubes. Label them with your initials, and place one in ice and one each in the 30°, 50°, and 70°C temperature baths. Wait five minutes, then take your enzyme to the baths and add 0.2 ml of enzyme to each tube. Wait about 1 minute and 45 seconds, then remove the tubes and take them to your desk, so that you can add the stopping reagent at exactly 2 minutes. Proceed as in the earlier measurements.

7. Metal-ion Dependence

Prepare three test tubes as shown in Table 4.5. After adding the enzyme, allow 2 minutes for each tube, and add 2.5 ml of stopping reagent. Develop, measure, and record the color intensities as before.

TABLE 4.5.

Metal-ion Dependence.

	Tube No.		
Add	1	2	3
MgC1$_2$, 50 μmoles/ml (A)	0.2[a]	—	—
MgC1$_2$, 5 μmoles/ml (B)	—	0.2	—
CaC1$_2$, 50 μmoles/ml (C)	—	—	0.2
Substrate (No. 1)	0.6	0.6	0.6
Enzyme	0.2	0.2	0.2

[a]Units are ml.

NOTES AND REVIEW QUESTIONS

Write a one-page (or shorter) summary of this experiment. Draw graphs depicting each series of measurements, always plotting the absorbance on the vertical axis, since this is the measured or independent variable, and plot the variable that you control by selecting reagents on the horizontal axis. Write a brief interpretation of each experiment, telling why it came out the way it did, referring to your text. Can you recognize any similarity between the reactions catalyzed by pyrophosphatase and by a protease?

REFERENCES

1. L. Heppel, "Inorganic Pyrophosphatase from Yeast," in S. P. Colowick and N. O. Kaplan, eds., *Methods in Enzymology* (Academic Press, 1955), II, 570.
2. M. Kunitz and P. W. Robbins, "Inorganic Pyrophosphatase," in P. D. Boyer, *The Enzymes* (Academic Press, 1961), V, 169.
3. S. Simmonds and L. Butler, "Alkaline Inorganic Pyrophosphatase of Maize Leaves," *Biochimica et Biophysica Acta,* 172 (1969), 150.

ANOTHER ENZYME, ALCOHOL DEHYDROGENASE

Substrate Affinity and Specificity, Various Types of Inhibition, Coenzyme Requirement

The procedures in this experiment will reveal some of the properties of the enzyme alcohol dehydrogenase (abbreviated ADH). This enzyme is found in a variety of tissues, and is conveniently purified from either mammalian liver cells or yeast cells. The enzyme from either source may be purified to homogeneity—that is, until no other protein is present—and then induced to crystallize. Alcohol dehydrogenase catalyzes the conversion of an alcohol (usually ethanol) to an aldehyde (usually acetaldehyde). The alcohol, on oxidation, looses reducing equivalents that must be transferred to a coenzyme—nicotinamide adenine dinucleotide (abbreviated NAD)—which in turn becomes reduced, to NADH. This reaction is described by the equation

$$CH_3CH_2OH + NAD \rightleftarrows CH_3CHO + NADH + H^+.$$

The coenzyme NAD may seem a bit less formidable if one recognizes that nicotinamide is another name for niacinamide (see Figure 5.1). Niacin is familiar from the small print on bread wrappers or cereal boxes, since it is a vitamin. Niacin must be included in the diet to supply part of the structure of NAD.

You may conveniently observe the activity of alcohol dehydrogenase by causing the products NADH + H⁺ to react with and reduce indophenol dye (see Figure 5.2). This dye is blue in the oxidized state and colorless in the reduced state (see Figure 5.3). With this assay, you will measure the characteristic affinity (K_M) of liver alcohol dehydrogenase for its substrate. You will compare the liver and yeast enzymes in terms of their substrate specificity—that is, their ability to catalyze the oxidation of various alcohols. You will test for inhibition of the enzyme activity by iodoacetate, which inhibits by reacting with an essential sulfhydryl group on the protein. You will observe inhibition by imidazole and by ortho-phenanthroline. The latter compound inhibits by removing an essential zinc ion from the protein, whereas imidazole prevents the substrate from approaching the active site of alcohol dehydrogenase. Finally you may easily demonstrate the essential role of NAD in the catalytic process.

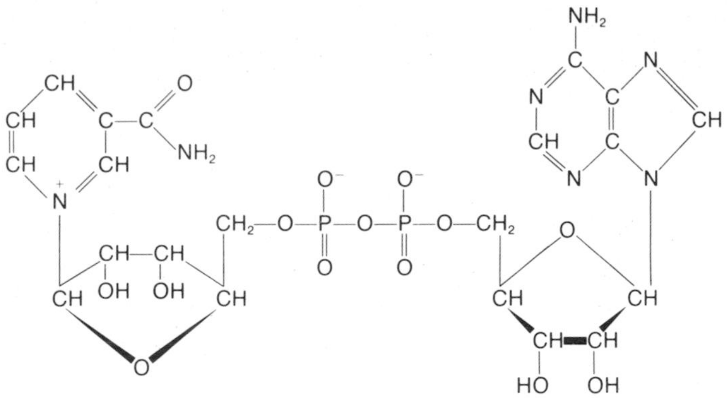

FIGURE 5.1.
Structure of the coenzyme NAD.

EXPERIMENTAL PROCEDURES

1. K_M for Ethanol with Liver Alcohol Dehydrogenase

An enzyme is characterized by its affinity for, or tendency to interact with, its substrate. A numerical expression for this affinity (the K_M or Michaelis constant) is obtained by measuring the rate of reaction at various substrate concentrations. An enzyme that works at top speed in catalyzing a reaction even at very low substrate concentrations must have a high affinity for that substrate.

Prepare the reaction mixtures summarized in Table 5.1 one at a time, withholding the enzyme (ADH)

TABLE 5.1.

K_M for Ethanol.

Add	Tube No.			
	1	2	3	4
NAD-dye stock No. 1	0.6[a]	0.6	0.6	0.6
Water	2.2	2.1	1.9	1.7
Ethanol ($1.6 \times 10^{-2}M$)	0.1	0.2	0.4	0.6
ADH	0.1	0.1	0.1	0.1

[a] Units are ml.

until the tube is ready to be put in the colorimeter. Add the enzyme, mix the tube thoroughly, and read the absorbance at 620 nm as promptly as possible. After three minutes, or after a 40 per cent decrease in the absorbance, take the 620 nm reading again and record it.

Plot values for the change in absorbance (initial minus final reading) versus the substrate concentration. The K_M is determined graphically as that substrate concentration which will give one-half the maximum reaction velocity. The reaction velocity is the change in color per unit time. The K_M is also determined graphically by plotting the reciprocal of the reaction velocity against the reciprocal of the substrate concentration; for this graph, the intercept on the x-axis is $-1/K_M$. Compare the values obtained by these two methods.

2. Substrate Specificity

Measure the relative effectiveness of five alcohols (methanol, ethanol, propanol, butanol, and isobutanol) as substrates for both the liver and the yeast enzyme. Use the volumes in Table 5.2 for all sub-

TABLE 5.2.

Substrate Specificity.

Add	All tubes
NAD-dye Stock No. 1	0.6 ml
Water	1.5 ml
Alcohol $1.6 \times 10^{-2}M$)	0.7 ml
Enzyme	0.2 ml

strates with each enzyme. Record the absorbance change at 620 nm after a three-minute incubation with the enzyme, or, if the reaction is slow, record the time required for a 30 per cent change in absorbance.

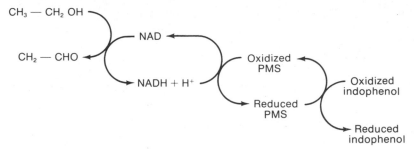

FIGURE 5.2.

Reaction sequence for measuring alcohol dehydrogenase activity.

3. Iodoacetate Inhibition

Make up reaction mixtures as shown in Table 5.3, withholding the ethanol. After adding the enzyme, allow 2 minutes for inhibitor-enzyme interaction. Then add the ethanol, and record the change in absorbance for three one-minute intervals.

4. Imidazole Inhibition

Set up reaction mixtures as shown in Table 5.4, and add the enzyme last, just before measurement, as in Parts 1 and 2. Record the absorbance changes over five one-minute intervals.

5. Orthophenanthroline Inhibition

Prepare reaction mixtures as shown in Table 5.5, and follow the procedures of Part 4. Record the absorbance changes over four one-minute intervals.

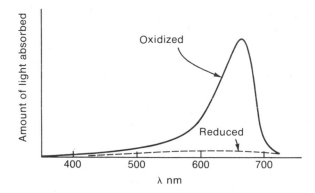

FIGURE 5.3.

Absorption spectra of oxidized and reduced indophenol dye.

TABLE 5.3.

Iodoacetate Inhibition.

	Tube No.			
Add	1	2	3	4
NAD-dye Stock No. 1	0.6[a]	0.6	0.6	0.6
Water	0.5	1.0	1.4	—
ADH (liver)	0.2	0.2	0.2	0.2
Iodoacetate	1.0	0.5	0.1	1.0
Ethanol	0.7	0.7	0.7	1.2

[a] Units are ml.

TABLE 5.4.

Imidazole Inhibition.

	Tube No.			
Add	1	2	3	4
NAD-dye-ethanol Stock No. 2	1.6[a]	1.6	1.6	1.6
Water	0.2	0.7	1.1	0.2
ADH (liver)	0.2	0.2	0.2	0.2
Imidazole	1.0	0.5	0.1	0.5
Ethanol	—	—	—	0.5

[a] Units are ml.

TABLE 5.5.

Orthophenanthroline Inhibition.

	Tube No.		
Add	1	2	3
NAD-dye-ethanol Stock No. 2	1.6[a]	1.6	1.6
Orthophenanthroline	0.5	0.5	—
Zinc chloride	—	0.5	—
Water	0.7	0.2	1.2
ADH (liver)	0.2	0.2	0.2

[a] Units are ml.

6. NAD Dependence

Set up reaction mixtures as shown in Table 5.6, and follow the procedure of Part 4. Record the absorbance changes over three one-minute intervals.

TABLE 5.6.
NAD Dependence.

Add	Tube No.		
	1	2	3
Dye-ethanol Stock No. 3	1.6[a]	1.6	1.6
NAD	—	0.2	0.4
Water	1.2	1.0	0.8
ADH (liver)	0.2	0.2	0.2

[a]Units are ml.

NOTES AND REVIEW QUESTIONS

1. Prepare the data from each of the six parts of this experiment in an intelligible graph or table.

2. Of what significance is the K_M value?
3. Which graphic method used to determine K_M do you think is more accurate? Why?
4. What is the effect of iodoacetate on enzyme activity? Does an increase in ethanol alter this condition? Is this inhibition competitive or noncompetitive?
5. In what way is imidazole inhibition different from iodoacetate inhibition?
6. Does the presence of orthophenanthroline increase or decrease the enzyme's activity? Does the addition of zinc chloride alter this?

REFERENCE

D. E. Koshland, Jr., "Correlation of Structure and Function in Enzyme Action," *Science,* 1963, p. 1533. Available in the Bobbs-Merrill Reprint Series from Howard M. Sams and Company, Indianapolis.

ATP, THE ENERGY CARRIER

Photosynthetic Phosphorylation, Bioluminescent Dephosphorylation, Transphosphorylation

Adenosine triphosphate is the key chemical mediator in all energy transformations within living cells. In green plants, the energy absorbed from sunlight is used to form a high-energy bond between inorganic phosphate and adenosine diphosphate to produce ATP. The chloroplasts are the pigment-containing structures within the plant cell where the photosynthetic phosphorylation of ADP occurs (see Figure 6.1). In animal cells, energy derived from the oxidation of reduced carbon compounds is used to drive the synthesis of ATP; this process occurs mainly in the mitochondria. ATP then supplies all the energy needed by the cell: for the synthesis of new cellular materials, for muscle contraction, for nerve conduction, even for light production by the firefly (see Figure 6.2).

In this experiment you will measure the synthesis of ATP by illuminated chloroplasts, conveniently, by measuring the disappearance of inorganic phosphate as it is used in photosynthetic phosphorylation to form ATP. You will observe how ATP produces light when it is mixed with an extract from firefly lanterns. The reversible transfer of phosphate from one high-energy compound to another illustrates an important energy transaction, analogous to depositing money in, and withdrawing it from, a savings account; you will study the reversible transfer of a phosphate group from creatine phosphate to ADP, catalyzed by the enzyme creatine kinase.

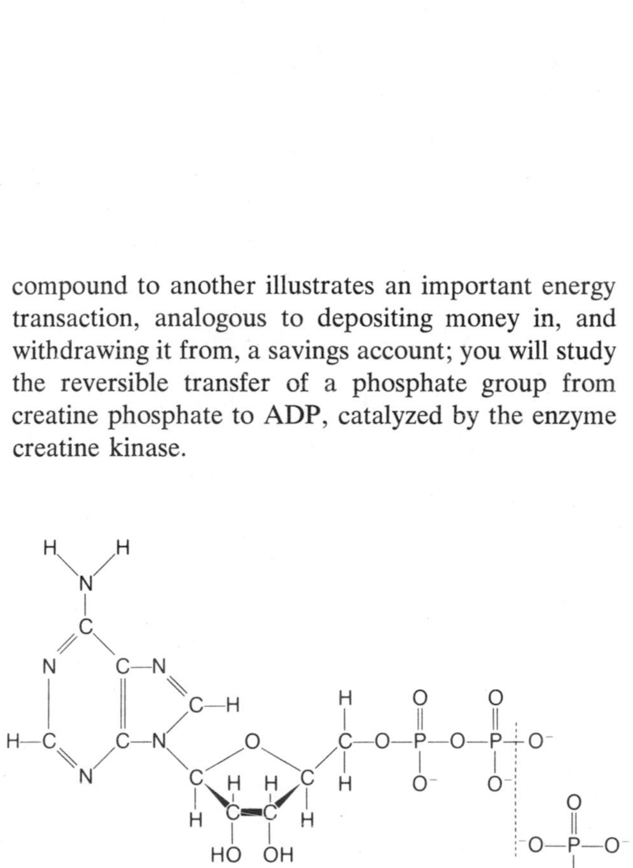

FIGURE 6.1.

The structure of ADP.

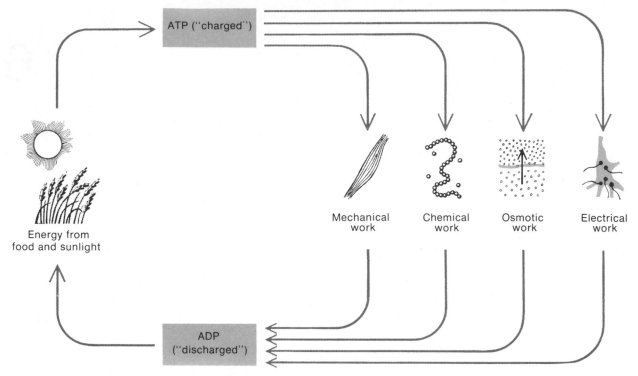

FIGURE 6.2.

Adenosine triphosphate (ATP), the common carrier of energy in animal and plant cells, is formed in the mitochondria and chloroplasts. It supplies energy for muscle contraction, protein synthesis, absorption or secretion against an osmotic gradient, and transfer of nerve impulses. "Discharged" adenosine diphosphate (ADP) thus formed is "charged" by solar or food energy. (From A. L. Lehninger, "How Cells Transform Energy." Copyright © 1961 by Scientific American, Inc. All rights reserved.)

EXPERIMENTAL PROCEDURES

1. Photosynthetic Phosphorylation

The synthesis of ATP from ADP and inorganic phosphate is one of the two reactions that convert light energy into chemical energy. (The other is the light-driven transfer of electrons from water, through a series of intermediates, to carbon dioxide; this reaction will be covered in the next experiment.) Chloroplasts, isolated from green plant cells, catalyze the photophosphorylation reaction which can be described in minimal detail by the equation

$$ADP + P_i \xrightarrow[\text{Mg}^{+2},\ \text{PMS}]{\substack{\text{light} \\ \text{chloroplasts}}} ATP.$$

PMS is phenazine methosulfate, which acts as a redox catalyst; it replaces a natural catalyst that is lost during isolation of the chloroplasts.

The chloroplasts to be used in your experiment are obtained from market spinach by the following procedure (see Figure 6.3). Twenty grams of leaves are ground in a mortar and pestle with a palm full of sand and about 40 ml of $0.4M$ sucrose solution. The grinding breaks the cells open, and the sucrose solution washes out the cell contents while preventing the subcellular structures from being disorganized by the osmotic shock that would occur if water were used instead of sucrose solution. The unbroken cells and fibers are removed by filtering through a double layer of cheesecloth. The homogenate is centrifuged at low speed to remove the nuclei and cell walls, which are larger than chloroplasts. The supernatant fluid from the first centrifugation is then centrifuged at higher speed to bring down the chloroplasts, leaving cytoplasmic enzymes, and the mitochondria and ribosomes, which are smaller than chloroplasts, in the supernatant liquid. The chloroplast pellet is resuspended in sucrose solution (about 8 ml) to give a chlorophyll concentration of 1 mg per ml.

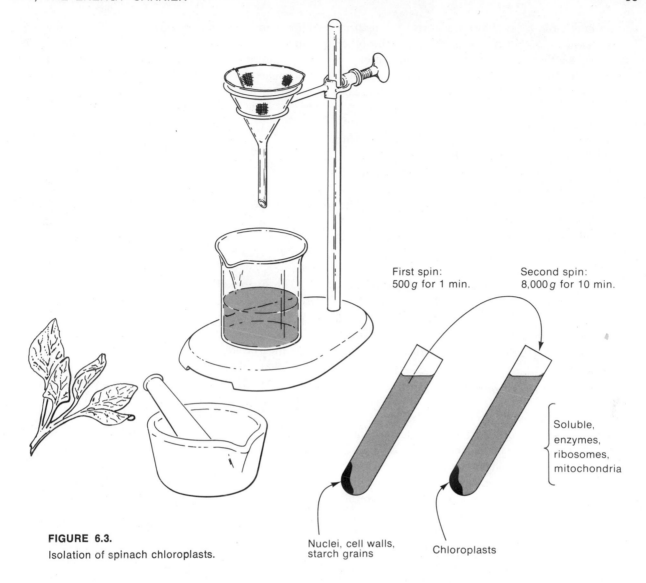

FIGURE 6.3.

Isolation of spinach chloroplasts.

First spin: 500 g for 1 min.

Second spin: 8,000 g for 10 min.

Soluble, enzymes, ribosomes, mitochondria

Nuclei, cell walls, starch grains

Chloroplasts

You will measure the amount of ATP synthesized by measuring the disappearance of inorganic phosphate from the reaction mixture. So that isolated chloroplasts may synthesize ATP, one must add ADP, P_i, Mg^{+2}, and phenazine methosulfate (PMS).

To provide light at constant temperature, fill a one-liter beaker with water to a depth of about 4 inches, and place it on a ring stand or tripod over a 150-watt lamp. Prepare the five reaction mixtures summarized in Table 6.1 in numbered, 25-ml Erlenmeyer flasks, adding the chloroplast solution *last*. Do not delay in performing the experiment once the reaction mixtures are prepared.

To flask number 5, add four drops of 20% trichloroacetic acid to denature the protein. (Caution! Avoid contact with skin or eyes. Your own proteins

TABLE 6.1.

Reaction Mixtures for Photosynthetic Phosphorylation.

Add	Flask No.				
	1	2	3	4	5
0.25M Tris buffer, pH 7.8, + 0.05M MgCl$_2$	0.1[a]	0.1	0.1	0.1	0.1
0.01M P_i buffer, pH 7.8	0.1	0.1	0.1	—	0.1
0.02M ADP, adjusted to pH 7 with NaOH	0.1	0.1	—	0.1	0.1
0.0005M PMS	0.1	—	0.1	0.1	0.1
H$_2$0	0.3	0.4	0.4	0.4	0.3
Chloroplasts containing 1 mg of chlorophyll per ml	0.1	0.1	0.1	0.1	0.1

[a] Units are ml.

can be denatured by trichloroacetic acid.) This flask will be used as a zero time control. Hold the other four flasks so that they just touch the surface of the water in the beaker, and turn on the light for five minutes. Gently move the flasks during the illumination period, so that their contents are well-mixed. At the end of this period, add four drops of 20% trichloroacetic acid to each flask. Carefully pour the contents of each flask into small test tubes with corresponding numbers. Spin the tubes for three minutes in the clinical centrifuge, balancing your five tubes against those of another student. From each tube, pour all of the supernatant, but none of the precipitated protein, into a large test tube with a corresponding number. Add a sixth tube, containing 1.0 ml of water, to this series as a reagent blank. Add 2.5 ml of the color reagent to each tube, and wait ten minutes for it to develop the phosphate color. Read the absorbance at 620 nm of each tube. Using your standard curve from Experiment 4, determine the amount of phosphate remaining in each reaction mixture.

2. Bioluminescent Dephosphorylation

The firefly produces light by using the high-energy phosphate of ATP to excite a special molecule, "luciferin," which then dissipates the energy by fluorescence—that is, by emitting light. The reaction is catalyzed by an enzyme called luciferase. Both luciferin and luciferase can be extracted from the carefully dried lanterns of fireflies. When called by the instructor, you will measure ATP concentrations by measuring the light produced when ATP is mixed with firefly extract. Place the ATP in a darkened and shielded tube in front of a photocell, which responds to different intensities of light just as a photographic exposure meter does—that is, by giving an electric current flux, which is translated into a meter reading or a pen trace on a chart. Inject firefly extract into the tube with a syringe to give rapid mixing. Use different concentrations of ATP, and let the machine record the flash heights on a strip-chart recorder. The flash height is proportional to the amount of ATP present. (Alternatively, you might use a more sensitive apparatus, the human eye, to observe the flash intensity in a totally darkened room.)

3. Muscle Enzyme Transphosphorylation

In muscle, creatine phosphate serves as a back-up reserve of the high-energy phosphate needed to phos-

phorylate ADP and provide, via ATP, the energy for moving the muscle. A key enzyme, creatine kinase, can shift the high-energy phosphate from creatine phosphate to ADP when there is much work to be done; the same enzyme can regenerate creatine phosphate when rest allows the formation of plenty of ATP.

$$\text{Creatine} + \text{ADP-P} \underset{}{\overset{\text{creatine kinase}}{\rightleftharpoons}} \text{Creatine-P} + \text{ADP}.$$

The reaction is reversible, and can be coaxed in one direction or the other. At pH 9, the reaction is pushed to the right, favoring creatine phosphate formation; at pH 5 to 7, the reverse reaction is favored. You will run the reaction in both directions, and assess its progress by two separate methods.

The first method employs the same reagents and color measurements you have used to determine the amount of inorganic phosphate in a sample. Although ATP is stable in the acid molybdate reagent used in the measurement of inorganic phosphate, creatine phosphate is not. The acid hydrolyzes (splits off) the phosphate from creatine phosphate. Thus, one can follow the transfer of phosphate from the acid-stable ATP to the acid-labile creatine phosphate by measuring the appearance of inorganic phosphate.

a. *Forward Reaction.* Make additions to three test tubes as summarized in Table 6.2. Wait two minutes

TABLE 6.2.
Creatine Kinase Forward Reaction.

Add	Tube No.		
	1	2	3
Creatine + MgC1$_2$	0.6[a]	0.6	0.6
ATP, 4 μmoles/ml	0.2	0.1	0.2
0.1M Tris buffer, pH 9	0.2	0.1	—
Creatine kinase, 80 μg/ml	—	0.2	0.2

[a] Units are ml.

after the addition of enzyme, then add 2.5 ml of the stop mixture. Allow 30 minutes for hydrolysis of phosphocreatine and color development. Use tube number 1 as the blank, and read the color at 620 nm. Using your standard curve for inorganic phosphate, compute the μmoles of creatine phosphate produced per minute per mg of protein for each tube.

b. *Standard Curve for Creatine Reverse Reaction.* The standard assay for creatine employs 2,3-butanedione and alpha-naphthol to form a complex that produces a pink color with creatine. In practice, the alpha-naphthol is added first, to stop the enzyme-catalyzed reaction from producing creatine. The alpha-naphthol is strongly basic and destroys the enzyme. Then the diacetyl (2,3-butanedione) is added, and the solution is diluted to a convenient volume.

To five test tubes, make additions as summarized in Table 6.3. Mix well and allow 30 minutes for the color to develop. On graph paper, plot μmoles of creatine against absorbance at 525 nm.

TABLE 6.3.
Standard Curve for Creatine.

	Tube No.				
Add	1	2	3	4	5
Creatine, 0.6 μmoles/ml	0.2[a]	0.4	0.6	0.8	1.0
H_2O	3.3	3.1	2.9	2.7	2.5
Alpha-naphthol	1.0	1.0	1.0	1.0	1.0
2,3-Butanedione	0.5	0.5	0.5	0.5	0.5

[a] Units are ml.

c. *Creatine-kinase-catalyzed appearance of creatine.* Make additions to three test tubes as summarized in Table 6.4. Wait two minutes after the addition of the

TABLE 6.4.
Appearance of Creatine Catalyzed by Creatine Kinase.

	Tube No.		
Add	1	2	3
ADP, 4 μmoles/ml	0.2[a]	0.1	0.2
$MgCl_2$, 25 μmoles/ml	0.2	0.2	0.2
Creatine phosphate, 25 μmoles/ml	0.2	0.2	0.2
Acetate buffer, pH 5.4, 100 μmoles/ml	0.4	0.3	0.2
Creatine kinase, 4 μgrams/ml	—	0.2	0.2

[a] Units are ml.

enzyme, and then add 1 ml alpha-naphthol, 0.5 ml of the diacetyl reagent, and 2.5 ml of H_2O, in that order. Place 1 ml of alpha-naphthol, 0.5 ml of diacetyl, and 2.1 ml of water in a tube to make a reagent blank. Mix well. Allow 30 minutes for color development, and read at 525 nm. Using the standard curve, compute the μmoles of creatine produced per minute per mg of protein for each tube.

NOTES AND REVIEW QUESTIONS

1. Tabulate the data from your measurement of photophosphorylation in terms of observed absorbance, μmoles of inorganic phosphate remaining, μmoles of inorganic phosphate disappeared, and μmoles of ATP formed. What can you conclude from the differences between the various reaction conditions used? Calculate the specific activity of spinach chloroplast phosphorylation from flask number 2 in terms of the μmoles of ATP formed per mg of chlorophyll per hour.

2. Make a graph from your chart record, plotting flash height on the vertical axis and ATP concentration on the horizontal axis. Now consider the units of concentration. A mole of a substance is m grams of that substance, where m is the numerical value of its molecular weight. A micromole (μmoles) is $1/1,000,000$ or 10^{-6} of a mole. A nanomole (nmole) is $1/1,000,000,000$ or 10^{-9} of a mole. Compare the sensitivity of the measurement of ATP formation by means of inorganic phosphate disappearance used in part 1 with that of the bioluminescent method used in part 2.

3. Describe by two equations the reactions used to (1) form creatine phosphate, and (2) measure the creatine phosphate formed. Use words, not exact chemical formulae. Explain the results you obtained in part 3 of this experiment, draw a proper creatine standard curve, and note the relative sensitivity of the creatine measurement compared with the measurements for inorganic phosphate and ATP.

REFERENCES

1. D. I. Arnon, "The Role of Light in Photosynthesis," *Scientific American,* November 1960. Offprint No. 75.
2. A. L. Lehninger, "How Cells Transform Energy," *Scientific American,* September 1961. Offprint No. 91.
3. W. D. McElroy and H. H. Seliger, "Biological Luminescence," *Scientific American,* December 1962. Offprint No. 141.

THE PHOTOSYNTHETIC REDUCING POWER OF ISOLATED CHLOROPLASTS

A Multienzyme System for the Transduction of Light Energy into Biological Reducing Power

The ability of green plants to convert carbon dioxide and water into reduced carbon and oxygen is the central fact of photosynthesis, and is the basis for all life on this planet, since the reduced carbon is then used for energy by animals (Experiment Ten deals with this use). The photosynthetic process depends on the light-driven synthesis of ATP, a reaction illustrated in the last experiment. In addition, the conversion of CO_2 to sugar is a chemical reduction in which hydrogen, as protons and electrons, is transferred from water to carbon dioxide. This transfer is driven by light energy and involves a complex series of enzymatic reactions, all of which occur in the chloroplast. Chloroplasts, isolated from leaf cells, catalyze the reduction of CO_2 in two stages. In the first stage, reducing power is transferred from water to NADP; it is a model of this reaction that you will examine:

$$H_2O + NADP \xrightarrow[\text{light}]{\text{chloroplasts}} NADPH + H^+ + \tfrac{1}{2} O_2.$$

Note that oxygen is the other product of this reaction.

Our indebtedness to green plants for this oxygen should be obvious. The reduction of an oxidized substance, such as NADP, with the concomitant production of oxygen by isolated chloroplasts, is called the Hill reaction. The $NADPH + H^+$ produced by the Hill reaction together with ATP generated in photophosphorylation, are then used by plants in an extended series of dark reactions to fix CO_2.

The parts of the experiment described here will show how chlorophyll, the main energy-absorbing pigment of the chloroplast, absorbs light selectively. Ferricyanide will be used as a convenient substitute for NADP in a manometric demonstration of oxygen production by the Hill reaction. The reduction of indophenol dye by illuminated chloroplasts is a sensitive colorimetric assay of activity, since the oxidized dye is an intense blue, but its reduced form is colorless. With the indophenol dye assay, you will measure the effects of chloroplast concentration, dye concentration, light intensity, wavelength (color) of light, and a specific inhibitor of photosynthesis on the rate of the Hill reaction.

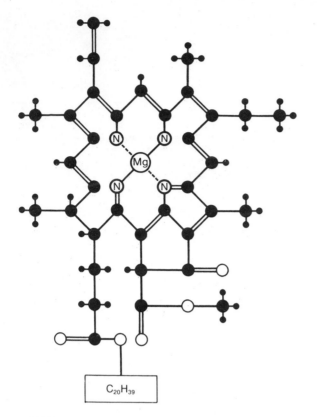

$C_{20}H_{39}$

FIGURE 7.1.

The structure of chlorophyll. (From A. L. Lehninger, "How Cells Transform Energy." Copyright © 1961 by Scientific American, Inc. All rights reserved.)

EXPERIMENTAL PROCEDURES

1. Absorption Spectrum of Chlorophyll

Place 2 ml of Stock A chloroplast suspension (0.04 mg of chlorophyll per ml) in a test tube, and add 8 ml of acetone from the burette in the hood. Allow the mixture to stand for five minutes; observe the cloudiness due to denatured protein, and filter the mixture into another test tube. Using a water blank, measure the absorbance of the chlorophyll extract at 20-nm intervals between 400 nm and 700 nm with the Spectronic 20 colorimeter. Record these sixteen absorbance (optical density) values and the wavelength at which each was obtained. When finished, let the chlorophyll extract stand in direct sunlight (or, if the day is cloudy, near the lamp in the hood) for the rest of the period. Before leaving, check the intensity of green color by eye and record your estimate.

2. Measurement of Oxygen Production by Illuminated Chloroplasts

Mix 1 ml of 0.001M potassium ferricyanide solution, 1 ml of 0.01M Tris buffer, pH 7.8, and 0.5 ml of Stock B chloroplasts (0.02 mg of chlorophyll) in a test tube. Place the tube in a beaker of water to control its temperature, and attach it to a ∪-tube manometer. Illuminate the reaction mixture with a 150-watt lamp placed about six inches from the beaker. Record the manometer response.

3. Effect of Chloroplast Concentration on the Rate of Dye Reduction

In a colorimeter tube, place 0.5 ml of Stock B chloroplasts and 2 ml of H_2O; this is your blank. In a second tube, place 0.5 ml of Stock B chloroplasts, 0.5 ml of Stock A dye solution (0.12 mg of 2,3,6-trichlorophenol indophenol per mil of 0.01M Tris buffer, pH 7.8), and 1.5 ml of H_2O. Using your chloroplast blank, read the absorbance of the second tube at 620 nm. Now hold the second tube 4 inches from the lamp, and illuminate it for 30 seconds. Read its absorbance again after illumination, and, by subtracting the reading after illumination from the reading before illumination, calculate the absorbance change. Repeat this procedure, using 1, 1.5, 2, and 2.5 ml of Stock B chloroplasts, adjusting the H_2O volume in each tube to give a final volume of 3.0 ml. The 0.5 ml of Stock A dye is equivalent to 0.1 micromole of dye. The Stock B chloroplasts contain 0.02 micromoles of chlorophyll per ml. Up to a point, increasing the chlorophyll should increase the light-dependent absorbance change. Record the data.

4. Effect of Dye Concentration on the Rate of Dye Reduction

Place 0.5 ml of Stock C chloroplasts (0.1 mg chlorophyll per ml) and 2.5 ml of H_2O in a colorimeter tube to use as a blank for all readings in this and subsequent sections. In an experimental tube, place the same amount of chloroplasts, 0.5 ml of Stock B dye reagent (it is one-half the concentration of Stock A dye), and 2 ml of H_2O. Measure the absorbance before and after 30 seconds of illumination. Repeat this procedure, varying the experimental reaction mixture by using 1, 1.5, and 2 ml of dye, adjusting the water for a final volume of 3 ml each time.

← ———— This is 4 inches. ————→

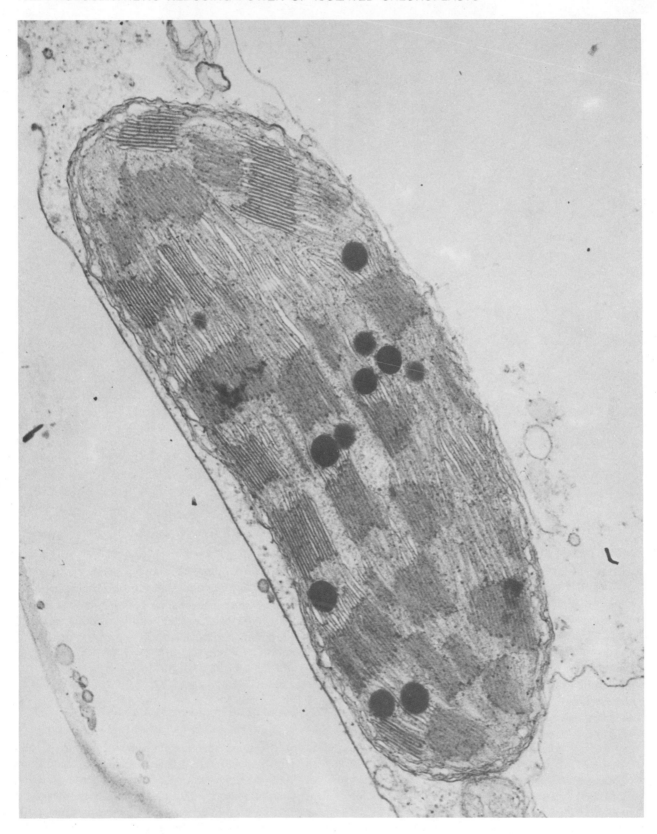

FIGURE 7.2.
An electron micrograph of the chloroplast from corn leaf. (Courtesy of J. Hall and F. L. Crane.)

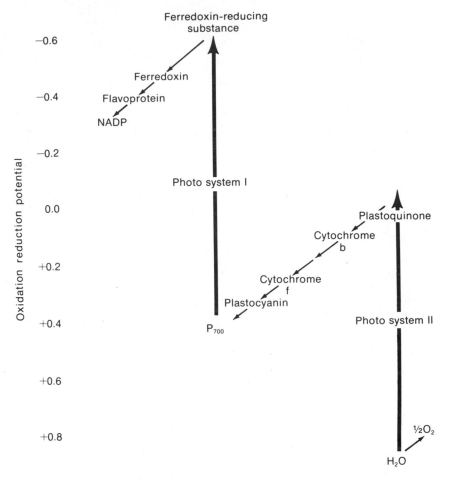

FIGURE 7.3.

The sequence of reactions catalyzed by illuminated chloroplasts.

5. Effect of Light Intensity

Using the blank from part 4, prepare an experimental tube containing 0.5 ml of Stock C chloroplasts, 0.5 ml of Stock A dye, and 2 ml of H_2O. Measure the absorbance before and after a 60-second illumination with the tube immersed in a beaker of water and two inches from the lamp. Repeat this procedure, at 4, 8, 16, and 20 inches from the lamp. Take care not to let your experiment be illuminated by another lamp that is less than 3 feet away.

6. Effect of Wavelength (Color) of Light

You have been provided with four light filters—red, green, blue, and yellow. Set them up one at a time,

four inches from the bulb, and, using a pair of tubes—blank and experimental—like those in part 4, determine the absorbance change for a 2-minute illumination with each filter, then with the yellow and blue filters combined. The absorption spectrum of each of the filters is given in Figure 7.4.

7. Effect of an Inhibitor

Using the same reaction mixture as in part 4, test the effects of 0.0, 0.5, 1.0, 1.5, and 2.0 ml additions of $0.000001M$ DCMU (1,1-dichlorophenyl dimethyl urea) solution on the Hill reaction activity, measured as the difference in absorbance before and after a 60-second illumination. This compound is one of the most effective commercial weedkillers.

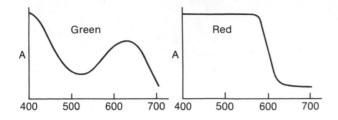

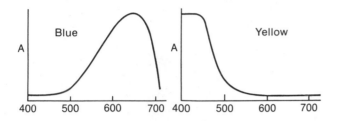

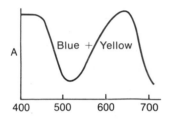

FIGURE 7.4.

Absorption spectra of cellophane filters. The scale on the horizontal axes gives the wavelength in nm.

NOTES AND REVIEW QUESTIONS

1. Using the data from part 1 of this experiment, plot absorbance on the vertical axis against wavelength on the horizontal axis to give an absorption spectrum of chlorophyll. Venture an explanation of why chlorophyll in acetone loses its color when exposed to strong light.

2. Give an interpretation of the manometer response in part 2.

3. Convert the data gathered in part 3 into the reaction rate—i.e., micromoles of dye reduced per micromole of chlorophyll per hour. Make a graph, plotting the reaction rate (on the vertical axis) against the amount of chlorophyll (on the horizontal axis). Give a common-sense interpretation of the shape of the curve.

4. Using the data from part 4, make a graph of the reaction rate against the dye concentration. Give a common-sense interpretation of the shape of the curve, referring to the usual enzyme-substrate relationship.

5. Using the data from part 5, make a graph of the reaction rate against the distance from the lamp. Again, give a common-sense interpretation of the shape of the curve. Why must you hold the reaction tube in water for this part of the experiment?

6. Using the data from part 6, make a table describing the rate of dye reduction with each filter (or combination of filters). Give a brief interpretation of each result, in terms of the absorption spectrum of chlorophyll (which you derived in answering question 1) and the absorption spectra of the filters.

7. Using the data from part 7, make a graph of the reaction rate against the amount of inhibitor present, and give a common-sense interpretation of the shape of the curve.

REFERENCES

1. J. A. Bassham, "The Path of Carbon in Photosynthesis," *Scientific American,* June 1962. Offprint No. 122.

2. R. P. Levine, "The Mechanism of Photosynthesis," *Scientific American,* December 1969. Offprint No. 1163.

CARBOHYDRATES

Structural Models and Chemical Tests for Sugars, and Some Enzymology of Carbohydrates

The carbohydrates are organic molecules that have a central role in metabolism and many important structural roles in the cell. The parts of this experiment are intended to help you become familiar with some of the significant chemical and biological properties of carbohydrates. You will build models of two simple sugars that illustrate the contrast between aldoses and ketoses. By combining these two hexose models to give a disaccharide, you will see the alpha and beta glycoside linkages. Next, a series of qualitative colorimetric tests will show you how various classes of sugars can be recognized and distinguished from one another. You will use an enzymatic method to measure the amount of glucose present in a sample, and you will measure the splitting of a polysaccharide into monosaccharide subunits by both chemical and enzymatic digestion.

EXPERIMENTAL PROCEDURES

1. Models of Simple Sugar Molecules

Figure 8.1 attempts to represent the pyranose and furanose rings of hexose in three dimensions. To un-

derstand the compounds represented in the figure, you must imagine that the plane of each ring is perpendicular to the plane of the paper on which the

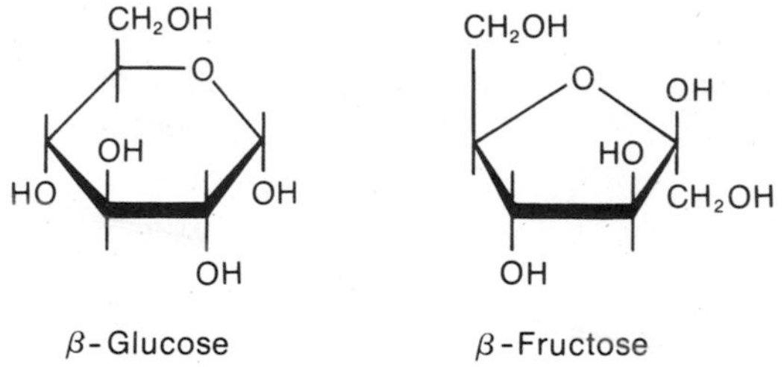

β-Glucose β-Fructose

FIGURE 8.1.

Structures of glucose and fructose.

ring is drawn. Thus, if you were looking down on the top edge of the page, the thicker lines would be pointing down and the thin lines would be pointing up (see Figure 8.2). The other groups attached to the ring would point either up or down from the plane of the ring.

To build a three-dimensional model of a hexose—which is much more satisfactory than pictures—you will use the Framework Molecular Models, which are often used in organic chemistry courses. The model parts have the following meanings.

Silver tetrahedron, center of a carbon atom.

Black tubing, carbon-carbon bond.

Black and red tubing, carbon-oxygen bond.

Red and white tubing, oxygen-hydrogen bond.

Black and white tubing, carbon-hydrogen bond.

To make glucose, lay out a hexagon and connect all the joints with tetrahedral connectors (see Figure 8.3). For simplicity, put this hexagon into chair form with the oxygen at the back; that is, with the red intersection in the back pointing up and the black intersection in the front pointing down. Now at carbon 5 (see Figure 8.4), add a carbon-carbon bond pointing up; put a silver tetrahedron on it, to represent carbon 6 (see Figure 8.5). To carbon 6 add a carbon-oxygen, with an oxygen-hydrogen attached by a linear connector. Add two carbon-hydrogens to the remaining positions on carbon 6.

To the remaining position on carbon 5, add a carbon-hydrogen, which will be pointing down.

On carbon 4, add a carbon-hydrogen pointing up and a carbon-oxygen, plus an oxygen-hydrogen pointing down.

On carbon 3, add a carbon-oxygen plus an oxygen-hydrogen pointing up, and a carbon-hydrogen pointing down.

On carbon 2, add a carbon-hydrogen pointing up, and a carbon-oxygen plus an oxygen-hydrogen pointing down.

On carbon 1, add a carbon-hydrogen pointing down, and a carbon-oxygen plus an oxygen-hydrogen pointing up. This gives the beta configuration to carbon 1.

Now make a model of galactose, which, you will remember, is an isomer of glucose. On galactose, at carbon 4, the carbon-hydrogen points down and the carbon-oxygen points up. The rest is like glucose.

Place the models side by side, with the glucose on the left and the galactose on the right. At the front of each model, you will see carbons 4, 3 and 2, from left to right. Make a sketch showing carbons 4, 3, and 2, with the -OH and -H substituents pointing down or up as in the models.

Now join the two hexoses together to make the disaccharide lactose, which is beta 1,4-linked glucopyranosyl galactopyranose. With the monosaccharide models still side by side and the glucose on the left, remove the oxygen-hydrogen piece from carbon 1 of glucose and the oxygen-hydrogen from carbon 4 of

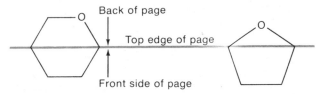

FIGURE 8.2.
Pyranose and furanose rings.

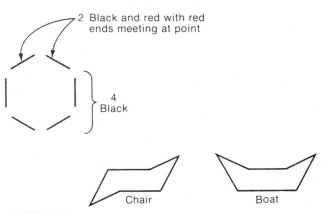

FIGURE 8.3.
Assembly of the pyranose ring and its possible conformations.

FIGURE 8.4.
Numbering of pyranose ring.

FIGURE 8.5.
Details at carbon number 6.

galactose, and join the two together, almost in (but above) the planes of the pyranose rings, with a linear connector. Had you started with an alpha configuration at carbon 1 of the glucose, with the carbon-hydrogen pointing up and the carbon-oxygen and oxygen-hydrogen pointing down, then the 1,4-linkage could be made alpha.

2. Chemical Characterization of Sugars

a. Seliwanoff's test. This test will distinguish between ketohexoses and aldohexoses. The ketohexoses produce more furfural derivatives than aldohexoses do in the presence of a strong acid. The furfural derivatives then react with resorcinol to give a red-colored compound. Pentoses will react to give a green or blue color.

Make additions to six test tubes as summarized in Table 8.1. Heat the tubes for exactly 60 seconds in the water bath. A red color is a positive test for a ketohexose. Record all the results.

TABLE 8.1.

Seliwanoff's Test.

	Tube No.					
Add	1	2	3	4	5	6
Seliwanoff's reagent (from burette)	9[a]	9	9	9	9	9
1% glucose	1					
1% sucrose		1				
1% galactose			1			
1% xylose				1		
1% fructose					1	
Unknown						1

[a] Units are ml.

b. Bial's test. This test is used to distinguish pentoses from hexoses. Pentoses give a blue-green color when heated with orcinol and ferric chloride in hydrochloric acid.

Make the same additions to six test tubes as in Table 8.1, but substituting 3 ml of Bial's reagent for the 9 ml of Seliwanoff's reagent. Mix and heat for exactly 60 seconds in boiling water. Record all the resulting colors.

c. Nelson's test. This test is used to detect the presence of reducing sugar in a sample. The reducing sugar (any aldose) reduces Cu^{2+} to Cu^{1+}, which forms a rust-colored precipitate (cuprous oxide, Cu_2O). The amount of cuprous oxide formed can be determined quantitatively by adding arsenomolybdic acid. The arsenomolybdate is reduced by the cuprous oxide, and the solution turns an intense blue color.

Make the additions to six test tubes as in Table 8.1, but substituting 1 ml of Nelson's reagent for the 9 ml of Seliwanoff's. Heat the tubes in boiling water for exactly twenty minutes. Then remove the tubes from the water bath, and add 1 ml of arsenomolybdate reagent. Shake until all the precipitate is dissolved. Add 5 ml of water to each tube. Record the colors.

3. Enzymatic Reactions With Sugars

a. Glucose standard curve. Glucose is an aldohexose that plays a central role in the metabolism of all cells. The "glucostat" test for glucose uses an enzyme that has absolute substrate specificity—glucose oxidase—to oxidize glucose. One of the oxidation products of the reaction is then reacted with a dye, and the resulting color can then be measured to determine the amount of glucose present in a sample. Since the quantity of glucose present in the blood or urine is of diagnostic value in treating diabetes, a simple colorimetric measurement of glucose is quite useful. The same test is used in the "Test Tapes" and "Clinistixs" sold to diabetics in any drugstore.

Make additions to seven test tubes as summarized in Table 8.2. Place all the tubes in ice. Get about 25 ml of the glucostat reagent from the stock solution, and keep it in ice. Add 2 ml of glucostat reagent to each tube as the tubes stand in ice. Then take all of the tubes to the 30°C water bath, and put them in as close to simultaneously as you can. Note the time. Allow the tubes to incubate for precisely 30 minutes. Then place all the tubes in ice again. Promptly add 1 ml of $1N$ HCl from the burette to each tube. Read and record the absorbance of light at 400 nm for each of the samples.

TABLE 8.2.

Glucose Standard Curve.

	Tube No.						
Add	1	2	3	4	5	6	7
Glucose (1 μmole per ml)	—	0.1[a]	0.2	0.3	0.4	0.5	—
Water	0.5	0.4	0.3	0.2	0.1	—	—
Unknown	—	—	—	—	—	—	0.5

[a] Units are ml.

b. Glycogen hydrolysis. Glycogen is a polysaccharide, a branched polymer of many glucose units. It can be broken down into individual glucose units under very mild conditions by an enzyme, amylase, found in saliva. Chemical splitting of glycogen requires a more violent acid hydrolysis at high temperature. In the polymer, the reducing aldehyde groups are masked in interglucose links, but on hydrolysis, the reducing sugar is freed and can reduce 3,5-dinitrosolicylate to give a visible color.

Take three test tubes, and place 5 ml of glycogen solution (0.64 mg per ml) in each. To the first tube, add 1 ml of 1N HCl, and heat it in a boiling water bath for 5 minutes. Remove it, and add 1 ml of 1.2N NaOH. Now add 1 ml of 3,5-dinitrosalicylate reagent. To the second tube add 1 ml of saliva. Allow the tube to stand for two minutes, then add 1 ml of 3,5-dinitrosalicylate reagent. To the third tube, add 1 ml of water and 1 ml of 3,5-dinitrosalicylate reagent. Boil all tubes for 5 minutes. The color indicates the presence of reducing sugar, glucose.

NOTES AND REVIEW QUESTIONS

1. Prepare the sketch showing carbons 4, 3, and 2 of glucose and galactose, as requested in part 1.
2. Prepare a table describing the color responses of various sugars to Seliwanoff's, Bial's, and Nelson's tests. Using this table, characterize your unknown. If you split out the sugar from ATP, how would it react in the above three tests?
3. Prepare the graph describing your glucose standard curve. Using the standard curve, calculate the glucose concentration of your unknown. Why is diabetic test tape best stored in the refrigerator?
4. Prepare a table describing the results of the experiment with glycogen. Interpret these results.

REFERENCES

1. G. Ashwell, "Colorimetric Analysis of Sugars," in *Methods in Enzymology* (Academic Press, 1957), III, 73.
2. H. V. Bergmeyer and E. Bernt, "Determination of Glucose with Glucose Oxidase and Peroxidase," in *Methods in Enzymatic Analysis,* (Verlag Chemie and Academic Press, 1963), p. 123.
3. J. D. Roberts and M. D. Caserio, *Basic Principles of Organic Chemistry* (Benjamin, 1965), Chapters 1 and 18.

THE CONSUMPTION OF GLUCOSE BY ANAEROBIC GLYCOLYSIS OR AEROBIC METABOLISM

The First Phase of Carbohydrate Breakdown

Most organisms use the same series of enzyme-catalyzed reactions to metabolize glucose. This reaction series, the Embden-Meyerhof pathway of glycolysis, is used by aerobic creatures like ourselves to convert glucose into pyruvic acid (see Figure 9.1). The pyruvic acid is then oxidized to carbon dioxide by another sequence, the Krebs cycle. In anaerobic creatures, the pyruvic acid resulting from glycolysis is subjected to some simple modification, and the products excreted from the cell. In yeast, the breakdown of sugar results in the production of ethyl alcohol and carbon dioxide. Since the production of fermented spirits from sugars has been a process of general interest for a very long time, the biochemistry of fermentation is well-understood. In this experiment, yeast will be incubated with glucose under a layer of mineral oil, which will exclude oxygen from the reaction environment. The glycolytic process yields carbon dioxide, which can be measured by the pressure increase on a manometer attached to the fermentation tube. Possibly you may be able to detect the aroma of ethyl alcohol at the end of the incubation period. Several inhibitors that suppress the activity of specific enzymes in the Embden-Meyerhof glycolytic sequence will be tested as inhibitors of carbon-dioxide production by fermenting yeast. Inhibition of the yeast fermentation is presumptive evidence that the target enzymes of the inhibitors are necessary participants in the fermentation process.

In a few tissues, glucose is used in another way. Instead of the Embden-Meyerhof glycolytic sequence, there is a direct oxidative degradation of glucose-6-phosphate. This pathway is called the phosphogluconate oxidative pathway, and involves the oxidative decarboxylation of hexose to pentose. Red blood cells from mammals use this alternative pathway exclusively. The oxidation of glucose-6-phosphate by red cells will be measured with a manometer. Since one carbon dioxide is produced for every two oxygens used, the reaction is more readily measured if the carbon dioxide is chemically removed from the reaction chamber. You will test this reaction sequence

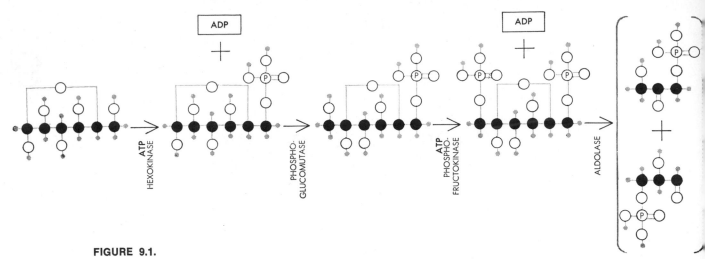

FIGURE 9.1.

Glycolysis, the process by which glucose (*first molecule*) is broken down into two molecules of pyruvic acid (*last molecule*), requires the catalytic aid of many enzymes (*light-face type*). Two molecules of ATP are needed to prime the process, but four are generated, yielding a net gain of two molecules of this energy-rich compound. Energy from glucose is also conserved by the reduction of the respiratory coenzyme DPN to DPNH (*sixth step*). The glycolytic reactions are reversible with the aid of appropriate enzymes. (From A. L. Lehninger, "Energy Transformation in the Cell." Copyright © 1960 by Scientific American, Inc. All rights reserved.)

with the glycolysis inhibitors, and, hopefully, find that they do not inhibit the phosphogluconate oxidative pathway.

EXPERIMENTAL PROCEDURES

1. Substrates for Yeast Glycolysis

Weigh out eight grams of Fleischmann's dry yeast, and suspend it in 100 ml of 0.02M sodium phosphate buffer (*p*H 6.8). Be sure to stir well immediately after adding the buffer, so that the yeast does not cake. Allow this suspension to incubate for about 15 minutes at room temperature. Take three test tubes, and place 1 ml of 0.2M sucrose in the first one, 1 ml of 0.2M glucose in the second, and 1 ml of 0.2M pyruvate in the third. Add 10 ml of the yeast suspension to each tube. Place 12 drops of mineral oil on top of the solution in each tube to make it anaerobic. Place the tubes in a water bath for 15 minutes, then take them one at a time, and connect each one to the manometer. Allow 30 seconds for temperature equilibration, then clamp off the vent hose and begin reading the manometer. Record the height of the manometer fluid in the left arm of the ∪-tube every minute for 5 minutes, or until the fluid reaches the top of the manometer.

2. Inhibitors of Glycolysis

Prepare three tubes as summarized in Table 9.1. Place 12 drops of mineral oil on top of the reaction mixtures and repeat the procedure used with the three previous tubes.

TABLE 9.1.

Glycolysis Inhibitors.

	Tube No.		
Add	1	2	3
0.2M sucrose	1.0[a]	1.0	1.0
1.0M iodoacetate	0.5	0.5	—
1.0M sodium pyruvate	—	1.0	—
1.0M sodium fluoride	—	—	0.5

[a]Units are ml.

3. Phosphogluconate Oxidative Pathway

Place 0.5 ml of freshly drawn, heparinized rat blood, 0.5 ml of 0.01M glucose-6-phosphate, and 0.1 ml of 0.01M phenazine methosulfate in a tube; insert a

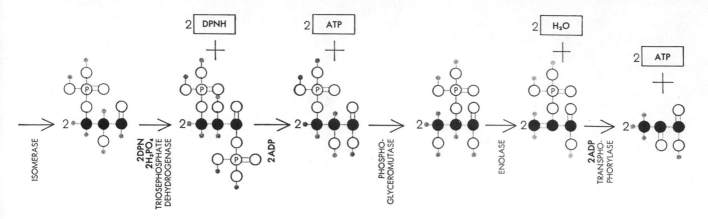

smaller tube containing a drop of 20% KOH (*Caution! Caustic!*) and a small paper wick (see Figure 9.2). This will absorb the carbon dioxide from the gas phase above the reaction mixture. The phenazine methosulfate (methylene blue could also be used) is added to facilitate the oxidation of reduced coenzymes within the red cell.

Measure the oxygen consumption as indicated by the height of the liquid in the left arm of the manometer every minute for 5 minutes. Repeat the mea-

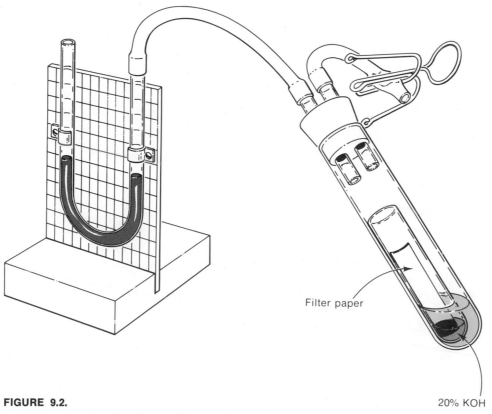

FIGURE 9.2.

∪-tube manometer with CO_2-absorbing trap.

surement, omitting the KOH trap, and then omitting the glucose-6-phosphate. Finally, test the activity of the complete reaction mixture in the presence of 0.5 ml of 1.0M sodium fluoride.

NOTES AND REVIEW QUESTIONS

1. Plot a graph of the height of the manometer fluid against the time for each of the reactions in part 1. Which metabolites appear to be used in anaerobic glycolysis?
2. Sodium fluoride is an inhibitor of enolase. Why does it stop carbon-dioxide evolution?
3. Prepare contrasting diagrams of the phosphogluconate oxidative pathway and the glycolytic pathway. Plot graphs describing the phosphogluconate oxidative pathway activity as measured under the various conditions in part 3.

REFERENCES

1. B. Axelrod, "Glycolysis," in O. M. Greenberg, ed., *Metabolic Pathways* (Academic Press, 3d ed., 1967), vol. I.
2. A. L. Lehninger, "How Cells Transform Energy," *Scientific American*, September 1961. Offprint No. 91.
3. H. G. Wood, "Significance of Alternate Pathways in Metabolism of Glucose," *Physiological Reviews*, 35, (1955), 841.

THE CONSUMPTION OF OXYGEN BY THE KREBS CYCLE AND BY POLYPHENOLASE

The Biochemical Basis of Respiration

The enzymes of the Krebs citric-acid cycle and the attendant enzymes of the respiratory chain are localized, within both plant and animal cells, in particulate structures called mitochondria (see Figures 10.1 and 10.2). In these structures the consumption of oxygen and the production of carbon dioxide commonly associated with breathing have their ultimate biochemical basis. Pyruvic acid derived from dietary carbohydrate is oxidized to carbon dioxide, and oxygen is reduced to water with the reducing power from the pyruvic acid (see Figure 10.3). This oxidation is the main point of energy release in metabolism, and so provides the main driving force for the synthesis of ATP. Thus mitochondria are the site of oxidative phosphorylation.

Mitochondria are conveniently prepared from fresh rat liver by mincing the liver into small pieces, then rinsing these small pieces twice with $0.25M$ sucrose in a ground glass homogenizer until they are pasty (see Figure 10.4). The homogenate is centrifuged at $600g$ for ten minutes to remove whole cells, large fragments of cell membrane, and nuclei. This pellet is discarded, and the supernatant is centrifuged at $10,000g$ for ten minutes to bring down the mitochondria. The mitochondria are resuspended in $0.25M$ sucrose (15 ml of $0.25M$ sucrose per 10 grams of liver).

You will use these isolated mitochondria to show that oxygen consumption is dependent on the organic acids of the Krebs citric-acid cycle. These measurements may be made with manometers, but you must trap the carbon dioxide that is produced in order to observe oxygen consumption. By using the KOH trap, you will be able to measure the oxygen consumption, since it will not be disguised by the carbon-dioxide production. You will test the competitive inhibitor—malonic acid—on the oxidation of succinic acid, and show the reversal of inhibition by excess substrate. You will use the uncoupler dinitrophenol (DNP) to demonstrate that the rate of oxygen consumption increases when the constraint of ATP synthesis has been released.

In many plant tissues, there is an oxygen consumption that is not caused by the Krebs cycle. The function of this plant enzyme system is not known with certainty, but it may, in part, be responsible for the

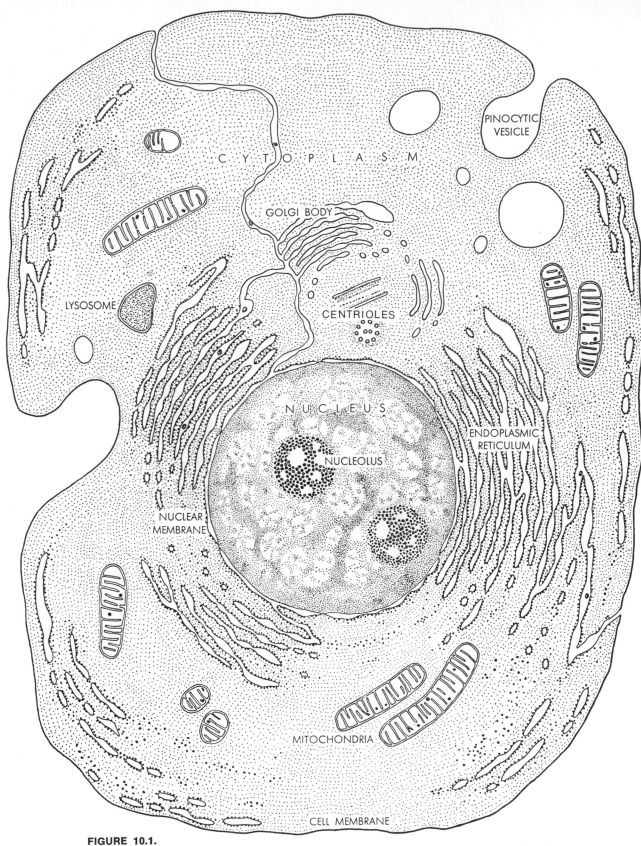

FIGURE 10.1.

Modern diagram of a generalized cell is based on what is seen in electron micrographs. The mitochondria are the sites of the oxidative reactions that provide the cell with energy. The dots that line the endophlasmic reticulum are ribosomes: the sites of protein synthesis. In cell division the pair of centrosomes, one shown in longitudinal section (*rods*), other in cross section (*circles*), part to form poles of apparatus that separates two duplicate sets of chromosomes. (From J. Brachet, "The Living Cell." Copyright © 1961 by Scientific American, Inc. All rights reserved.)

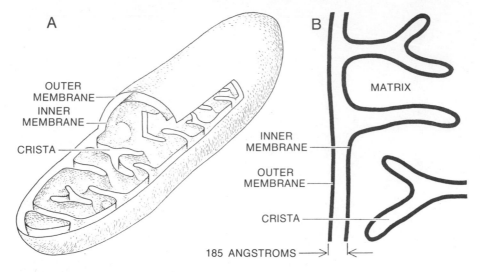

FIGURE 10.2.

Structure of mitochondrion is basically that of a fluid-filled vessel with an involuted wall (*a*). The wall consists of a double membrane (*b*), with infoldings of the inner one forming cristae. Each membrane is apparently constructed of a layer of protein. (From A. L. Lehninger, "How Cells Transform Energy." Copyright © 1961 by Scientific American, Inc. All rights reserved.)

production of oxidized phenolic compounds, which are abundant in plant tissues. Such enzymes—phenolases—are responsible for the darkening of cut fruit. The reactions catalyzed by phenolase introduce oxygen into an organic structure without concomitant production of carbon dioxide. The phenolases are copper proteins, and can be inhibited by certain chelating agents, which are organic compounds that bind copper very avidly and thus make it unavailable for its coenzyme role with phenolase.

You will use sections of apple tissue to demonstrate that, when the interior tissue is exposed, phenolase will use the oxygen made available to it to oxidize phenolic substrates in the cells. The measured rate of oxygen consumption will increase only slightly, if at all, in the presence of a KOH trap for removal of carbon dioxide. You will test inhibition of the reaction by a copper-binding reagent.

EXPERIMENTAL PROCEDURES

Each student will be supplied with 15 ml of a mitochondria suspension for this experiment. Keep it on ice. As soon as you get it, place 0.5 ml of it in a test tube, along with 1 ml of 0.1*M* phosphate buffer, *p*H 7.4, and a KOH trap. Swirl this tube in a water bath for a minute to equilibrate the temperature, and

attach it to a manometer. Close off the vent and observe. This oxidation, in the absence of added substrate, is due to endogenous substrates that have not been removed by the isolation procedure.

Take your entire mitochondrial prep and incubate it in the 30°C water bath for 12 minutes. This should allow the endogenous substrate to be used up. Check this by repeating the measurement with mitochondria, buffer, and the KOH trap as before. Then return the mitochondria to ice.

Since such endogenous respiration would vitiate the experiment, you must check for endogenous respiration before each part of the experiment. That is, you must place the mitochondria and the KOH trap in the tube before adding the other reagents, and attach it to the manometer. If any respiration is noted, allow the tube to stand, checking the respiration every few minutes until the rate is no more than 1 mm per minute. Then add the other reagents and continue with the experiment.

1. Oxidation of Krebs Cycle Intermediates

Place 1 ml of mitochondria in a test tube, allow a minute for equilibration in the water bath, drop in the KOH trap, and check for endogenous respiration. When none is present, add 1 ml of 0.5*M* sodium

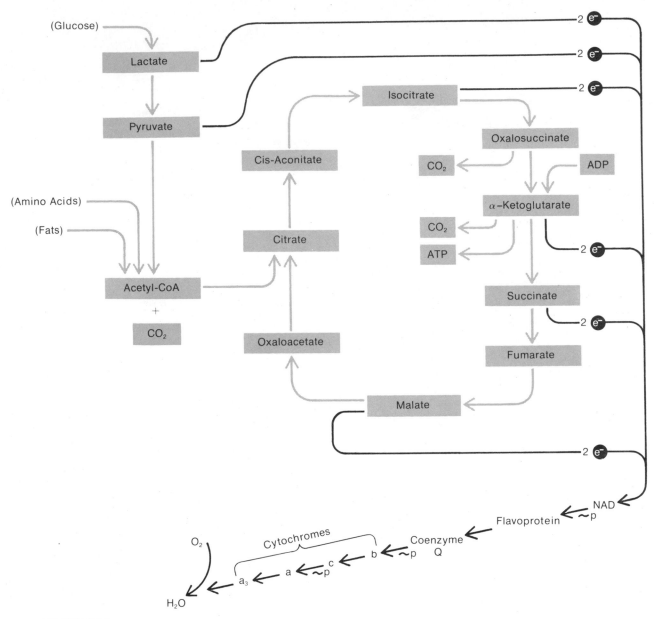

FIGURE 10.3.

The Krebs citric-acid cycle and the respiratory chain. (From A. L. Lehninger, "How Cells Transform Energy." Copyright © 1961 by Scientific American, Inc. All rights reserved.)

succinate. Be sure to pipette it into the mitochondria, and *not* into the KOH trap. Attach the manometer, clamp off the vent and record the millimeters of dye movement per minute for five minutes. Now pour off the reaction mixture carefully and recover the KOH trap.

Repeat the above procedure with citrate. Then, repeat the citrate and succinate procedures, but omitting the KOH trap.

2. Malonate Inhibition

Place 1 ml of mitochondria in a test tube and check the endogenous respiration. Then add 0.8 ml of buffer, 0.2 ml of $0.5M$ succinate, and a freshly prepared KOH trap. Attach the manometer and record the readings every minute for five minutes.

In a fresh tube repeat the above procedure with 1 ml of mitochondria, 0.2 ml of succinate, 0.4 ml of

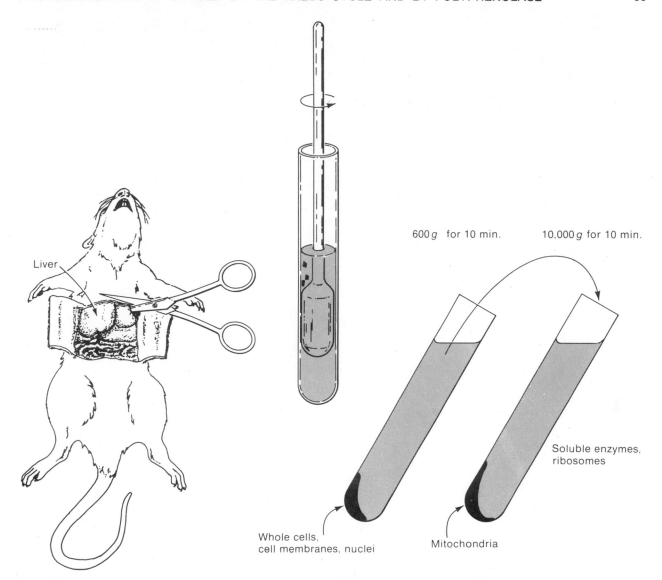

600 g for 10 min.   10,000 g for 10 min.

Soluble enzymes, ribosomes

Liver

Whole cells, cell membranes, nuclei

Mitochondria

FIGURE 10.4.
Isolation of rat-liver mitochondria.

malonate ($2M$), and 0.4 ml of buffer. After recording the rate of oxygen consumption for five minutes, remove the manometer, and pipette in 1 ml of $0.5M$ succinate. Reattach the manometer and record the readings every minute for five minutes.

3. DNP Uncoupling

In a test tube, place 1 ml of mitochondria, 0.7 ml of buffer, and a fresh KOH trap. After checking for the cessation of endogenous respiration, add 0.2 ml

of succinate and 0.1 ml of $0.01M$ DNP (2,4-dinitrophenol). Attach to a manometer, and record readings every minute for five minutes. Compare with the results from the first measurement in part 2.

4. Detergent Inhibition

Place 1 ml of mitochondria in a test tube with 0.5 ml of 10% Triton X-100, and allow it to stand for 10 minutes. Then add 1 ml of $0.5M$ succinate, attach to the manometer, and observe as before.

5. Apple Polyphenolase

Pierce through a ripe apple three times with a Number One cork borer, and put all three cores withdrawn by the borer into a test tube. Attach the tube to a manometer and record the fluid level of the open arm for five one-minute intervals. Repeat this procedure with fresh apple tissue, using a KOH trap. Repeat this procedure with cores that have been pretreated for five minutes by soaking them in $0.1M$ sodium diethyl dithiocarbamate, a copper chelator.

NOTES AND REVIEW QUESTIONS

1. Why are the mitochondria prepared and stored in $0.25M$ sucrose?

2. Make graphs of each of the experiments. Explain the responses of the mitochondria under each of the various conditions.
3. Interpret the malonate inhibition and its reversal.
4. Interpret the DNP effect.
5. Why does Triton, a powerful detergent, have the observed effect?
6. From common experience, what color would you expect the concentrated, accumulated products of polyphenolase to have?

REFERENCES

1. D. E. Green, "The Mitochondrion," *Scientific American,* January 1964.
2. A. L. Lehninger, "How Cells Transform Energy," *Scientific American,* September 1961. Offprint No. 91.

LIPIDS

Models, Chromatographic Separation, and Chemical Identification

Lipids are biologically important compounds that are distinguished by their insolubility in water. Lipids function as nutrient reserves (the depot fats); as structural material within the membranes; as regulatory substances (steroid hormones); and as energy collectors (photosynthetic pigments). Models of some lipid molecules will illustrate the general characteristics of these compounds (see Figure 11.1).

You will do a chromatographic separation of lipids, since, in studying any class of compounds, you must first be able to separate the individual members of the class from one another. The separation technique can often be used to identify individual compounds by making comparisons with standards. Thin-layer chromatography is the technique most often used in lipid separations. It is similar in operation to the paper chromatography you used for separation and identification of amino acids in Experiment One, but is different in principal, in that separations are achieved by differences in the strength of binding or absorption of a compound to a layer of silica gel or some other solid, rather than by partition of the compound between two different solvents.

Thin-layer chromatography plates are prepared by coating a glass or plastic supporting sheet with a layer of absorbent material. Solutions of the compounds to be separated are spotted on the plates, and allowed to dry. The plates are placed in a chromatography tank containing the appropriate solvent, in which the individual compounds separate on the basis of their relative affinities for the absorbent and their relative solubilities in the solvent. When the solvent has risen far enough, the plate is taken out, and the solvent allowed to evaporate from it. The plate is sprayed with color-developing reagents to detect the positions of colorless lipids, and the R_f values of the compounds recorded. You will use this technique to separate and identify a variety of lipids, including some plant pigments.

In addition to chromatography, lipids can be characterized chemically by, for example, a specific colorimetric test for the recognition of cholesterol, and by

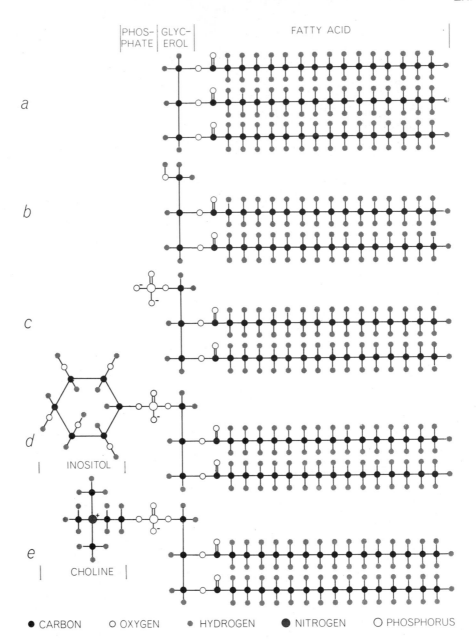

FIGURE 11.1.

Structure of five lipids, triglyceride (a), diglyceride (b), phosphatidic acid (c), phosphatidyl inositol (d), and phosphatidyl choline, or lecithin (e), is illustrated. Long groups to right are fatty acids. Names of groups to left are between short vertical brackets. (From L. E. Hokin and M. R. Hokin, "The Chemistry of Cell Membranes." Copyright © 1965 by Scientific American, Inc. All rights reserved.)

a quantitative iodination of lipids to determine the amount of unsaturated fat present. The recognition of cholesterol and the measurement of its concentration in blood has become an important tool in the diagnosis of heart disease. The measurement of unsaturated fatty acid content of lipids is useful in studying the origin, function, and possibly the dietary effects of various lipids.

EXPERIMENTAL PROCEDURES

1. Lipid Models

Several trays, each containing Prentice-Hall Framework Molecular Model atoms and bonds, will circulate through the laboratory. When you get the tray, make a model of a mixed triglyceride containing stearic, oleic, and palmitic acids, in the order alpha stearyl, beta oleyl, gamma palmityl triglyceride. Sketch the model, then disassemble it, and assemble a phosphatidyl ethanolamine containing myristic and lauric acids. Sketch this model, note the isomerism possible with the positioning of the fatty acids, then disassemble the model, and pass it on.

The pieces are:

Silver tetrahedron,
  center of a carbon or nitrogen atom;
Brass trigonal bipyramid,
  center of a phosphorus atom;
Black tubing,
  carbon to carbon bond;
Black and red tubing,
  carbon to oxygen bond;
Red and white tubing,
  oxygen to hydrogen bond;
Black and white tubing,
  carbon to hydrogen bond;
Blue and white tubing,
  nitrogen to hydrogen bond;
Blue and black tubing,
  nitrogen to carbon bond;
Purple and red tubing,
  phosphorous to oxygen bond.

2. Chromatographic Separation of Lipids

In order to conserve thin-layer plates, two students will share one plate. Each student is to separate five known lipids (reporting the R_f values as defined in Experiment One). The component(s) of an unknown will be identified from the R_f values of the standards.

All the solutions to be spotted will be supplied with capillary tubes as 1% solutions in chloroform; they are:

(1) cholesterol,
(2) cholesterol acetate,
(3) stearic acid,
(4) cholesterol palmitate, and
(5) tributyrin.

Hold the sample in the capillary pipette simply by holding a finger over the upper end of the tube after dipping it into the sample solution. Spot the samples by gently touching the silica gel layer a few cm from the bottom edge of the plate, with the tip of the capillary pipette and allowing a small drop of liquid to run on to the gel. Space the spots by laying the plate on the guideline (Figure 11.2). After all the solutions have been spotted and the plate is dry, place the plate into a chromatography tank that contains the following solvent: n-hexane, diethyl ether, and acetic acid, in the ratio of 70:30:1. Allow the solvent to come within three centimeters of the top of the plate (about 1 hour). Remove the plate, and dry it in the hood. Pour the solvent from the tank into a waste beaker. Have the instructor spray the plate with an 0.05% solution of Rhodamine G in 70% ethanol. Observe the plate under long wavelength UV light. (*Caution:* your eyes can be damaged by looking at a UV lamp for too long.) Circle the fluorescent spots, sketch the chromatogram, tabulate the R_f's for each of the standards, and identify the unknown(s).

Many of the colored substances in plant materials are classified as lipids, because of their insolubility in water and their solubility in organic solvents. You will be provided with organic solvent extracts of four plant materials, such as spinach leaves, a blue-green alga, carrot root, and corn seed. The extracts were prepared by grinding the material in a mixture of 1 part of acetone to 2 parts of diethyl ether. The extract was filtered and dried over solid anhydrous magnesium sulfate. The solution was then concentrated under vacuum in dim light. (Why? See experiment on Hill reaction).

Spot a half-inch line, as narrow as possible, one inch from the bottom of the plate, then repeat in the next space by drawing the line three times over, so there will be two different concentrations of each extract (see Figure 11.3).

Now pour enough solvent (isooctane, acetone, and ether, in the ratio 2:1:1) into the tank to give about a quarter-inch-deep pool in the bottom, and develop this chromatogram. When the development is complete, dry the plate, and sketch the distribution of

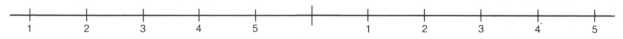

FIGURE 11.2.
Guideline for spotting.

| spinach 1X | spinach 3X | alga 1X | alga 3X | carrot 1X | carrot 3X | corn 1X | corn 3X |

FIGURE 11.3.
Pattern for spotting of extracts

colored compounds. Have the plate sprayed with Rhodamine G, and look at it under the UV light. Label any newly visualized compounds, and sketch the results.

3. Liebermann-Burchard Reaction

This reaction is useful for identifying and measuring sterols (see Figure 11.4). Addition of acetic anhydride and sulfuric acid to a sterol sample will produce

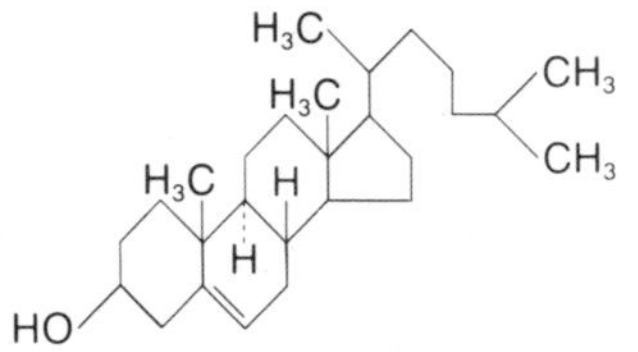

FIGURE 11.4.
The structure of cholesterol.

a series of color changes within five minutes. The initial color is pink, the final color dark blue-green. Fats that do not contain sterols will not give any color changes. The following five lipids will be tested: cholesterol, tributyrin, cholesterol palmitate, stearate, and cholesterol acetate (1 mg per ml of chloroform). Place 3 ml of each lipid sample in a separate test tube. Add 10 drops acetic anhydride (*caution*: do not inhale or get on skin) and 2 drops concentrated sulfuric acid (*caution*: causes severe burns) to each tube. Shake gently and allow to stand for 5 minutes. Note the color formation. Which lipids are sterols? What colors are produced by reaction of nonsterols?

4. Iodine Number

The iodine number is defined as the number of grams of iodine consumed by the unsaturated fatty acids present in a 100 gram sample of fat. Unsaturated fatty acids, either free or combined, react with iodine. The saturated fatty acids contain adjacent carbon atoms with one covalent bond and one electron pair between them (as in Figure 11.1). In contrast, unsaturated fatty acids have one or more pairs of adjacent carbon atoms with two covalent bonds and two electron pairs between them. The extra electron pair is capable of reacting with two iodines: thus, the greater the unsaturation in a fat sample, the more iodine consumed. A standard amount of iodine is mixed with the fat, and after the reaction, the unused iodine is measured by titration with sodium thiosulfate solution.

You will measure the relative degree of unsaturation of 0.3% linseed oil and 0.3% lard. Place 10 ml of a lard sample in a 250-ml Erlenmeyer flask, and 10 ml of a linseed-oil sample in another such flask. Both have been dissolved in CCl_4, carbon tetrachloride, which is *never* pipetted, since the fumes can induce cirrhosis of the liver. Now, add 10 ml of a $0.1N$ iodine monobromide solution to each flask (*caution*: do not inhale or get on skin). Shake the flasks gently, stopper, and set in a dark place for 30 minutes. Add a few crystals of potassium iodide to each flask, and then add $0.1N$ sodium thiosulfate slowly, stirring until the solution becomes colorless. Record the volume of thiosulfate used.

NOTES AND REVIEW QUESTIONS

1. Make the sketches of the lipid models. Redraw the triglyceride with a trans double bond instead of the usual cis.
2. Make sketches of the lipid chromatograms, with identifications, and a table of the R_f values of the standards. Identify the unknown.
3. Make a table describing the results of the Lieberman-Burchard tests, and interpret them.
4. Interpret the results of your measurement of the iodine number. Judging from the television advertising of margerine, would you expect animal or vegetable fats to have a higher iodine number?

REFERENCES

1. L. F. Fieser, "Steroids," *Scientific American*, January 1955. Offprint No. 8.
2. L. E. Hokin and M. R. Hokin, "The Chemistry of Cell Membranes," *Scientific American*, October 1965. Offprint No. 1022.
3. H. H. Strain and J. Sherma, "Modification of Solution Chromatography Illustrated with Chloroplast Pigments," *J. Chem. Education*, 46, no. 8 (August 1969), 476.

LIPIDS

Enzymology and the Role
of Lipids in the Cell

Mammalian metabolism of lipids begins with the breakdown of ingested dietary lipids by enzymes released from the pancreas into the digestive tract. You will use a preparation of pancreatic enzymes to hydrolyze triglycerides to glycerol and free fatty acids, and will measure the reaction quantitatively by titrating enough base to neutralize the acid released by the enzymatic hydrolysis (see Figure 12.1). "Excess acidity" can be measured by the color change of an indicator dye or by an electrode that responds to change in pH (change in the hydrogen-ion concentration; note that hydrogen ions are released in this reaction).

In plants, the unsaturated fatty acids released from triglycerides are often attacked by the enzyme lipoxidase, which oxidizes and ultimately breaks the double bonds. The activity of this enzyme is easily measured by using beta carotene, a yellow lipid. Lipid peroxides produced by lipoxidase react with beta carotene to destroy its visible color.

To illustrate the role of lipids in membrane structure, you will measure the effects of phospholipase on the membrane of the red blood cell. Phospholipase degrades the lecithin in the red cell membrane, causing the cell to burst.

EXPERIMENTAL PROCEDURES

1. Colorimetric Assay
of Lipase Activity

Take a 50-ml beaker containing 0.5 grams of a permanent emulsion of coconut-oil lipids, and dissolve the lipids in 6 ml of distilled water. As a general rule, lipids are exceedingly difficult to dissolve in water. Frequently it is necessary to use a detergent to dissolve them, as you may have noticed when washing dishes. Here the lipids are dispersed as tiny droplets that mix well with water but may give it a milky appearance. Add 10 ml of $0.05M$ NH_4Cl–NH_4OH buffer, pH 8, dropwise with shaking, and then add 10 ml of $0.1M$ $CaCl_2$ in the same manner. Calcium ions will form a salt with the free fatty acid, which facilitates the hydrolysis of triglycerides by lipase.

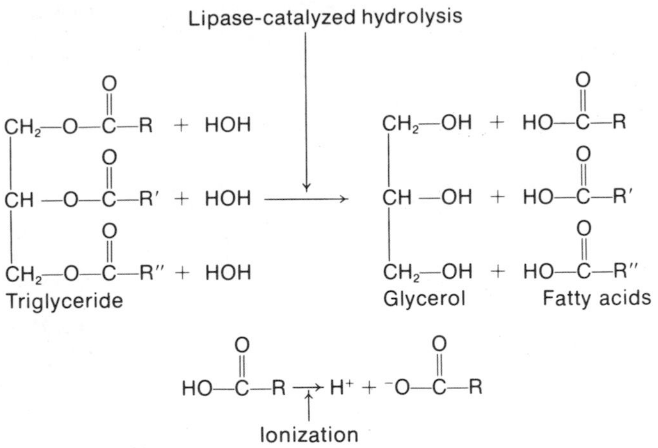

Lipase-catalyzed hydrolysis

FIGURE 12.1.

Hydrolysis of a triglyceride.

Now add 1 ml of 1% phenolphthaline with shaking. This indicator dye will change color when the reaction mixture becomes acidic because of the release of fatty acids.

Put the reaction beaker in a 37°C water bath, and add 5 ml of lipase solution. Mix, and immediately withdraw a 5-ml sample for titration.

Titrate each sample as follows. Transfer the 5-ml aliquot of reaction mixture to a 200-ml beaker, and add 75 ml of a 9-to-1 mixture of 95% ethanol ether. Note the initial liquid level on a burette containing $0.02N$ standardized KOH solution, and add this base, drop by drop, until the phenolphthaline turns faint pink. Note again the liquid level in the burette, and record the amount of base needed to neutralize the acid in the sample as indicated by the phenolphthaline color change.

Allow the reaction mixture to incubate at 37°C with occasional swirling. Maintain the pink color of the phenolphthaline by periodically adding small amounts of $1N$ NH$_4$OH from the dropping bottle, otherwise the reaction mixture will become too acidic for the enzyme to continue functioning. Withdraw 5-ml aliquots from the reaction mixture at 15, 30, 45, and 90 minutes after the addition of enzyme and titrate each sample immediately.

2. *pH* Meter Assay of Lipase Activity

An alternative method for measuring lipase action is to use the *pH* electrode. The electrode allows selective penetration of hydrogen ions through a glass membrane from the surrounding solution. Once inside the electrode, the hydrogen ions react to generate an electrical current, which is translated into a meter reading. As in part 1, prepare the mixture of lipids and calcium chloride, but do not add the buffer or lipase yet. Add a magnetic stirring bar. Put the beaker on the magnetic stirrer next to the *pH* meter, and carefully transfer the electrodes from the beaker of water in which they are stored to the stirring reaction mixture (see Figure 12.2). Do *not* allow the electrode to be scratched or chipped or to dry out; such mishaps would ruin the properties of the glass membrane.

Measure the *pH*, and adjust it to *pH* 8.2 by adding $0.02N$ KOH from the burette. Start the reaction by adding 5 ml of lipase solution, and note the time in seconds. The *pH*, as measured on the meter, should begin to drop. When the meter needle reaches 7.7, note the time in seconds, and add enough KOH to raise the *pH* to 8.2 again. Record the burette reading. When the needle again reaches 7.7, record the time required for the *pH* change. Add more KOH to again raise the *pH* to 8.2, and record the final burette reading. A stopwatch (or at least a clock with a second hand) would probably be very helpful during this procedure.

3. Colorimetric Assay of Lipoxidase Activity

Lipoxidase is assayed by measuring the bleaching of beta carotene. First mix 9 ml of the carotene substrate solution with 2.5 ml of $0.1M$ phosphate buffer, *pH* 6.8. Transfer 3 ml of the buffered substrate to a colorimeter tube, and measure the absorbance at 425 nm. Now add 0.1 ml of lipoxidase, mix well, and record the absorbance every 10 seconds. After several

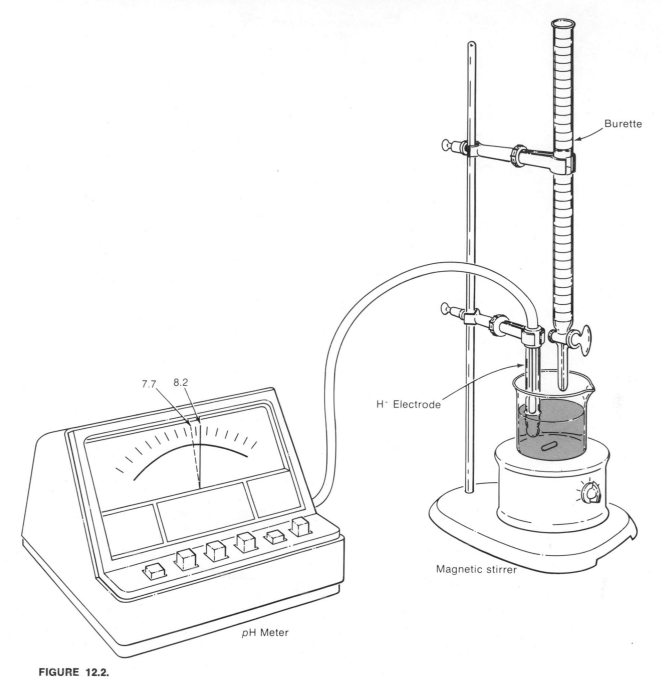

FIGURE 12.2.

Arrangement for *p*H-meter titration of lipase-catalyzed acid production.

minutes of incubation, make a visual comparison of the solution in the colorimeter tube to the original substrate solution.

4. Enzymatic Breakdown of Membrane Lipids

Phospholipids such as phosphatidyl ethanolamine—lecithin—are part of cell membranes, and are broken down by a family of enzymes called phospholipases. In this experiment, you will observe the action of phospholipase A, or lecithinase. This enzyme hydrolyzes lecithin to produce lysolecithin and a free fatty acid (see Figure 12.3). Lysolecithin is a very potent hemolyzing agent. It acts as a detergent, and disrupts the lipid structure of the red-cell membrane, causing the cells to lyse or burst open. The contents of the cell are emptied into the surrounding solution

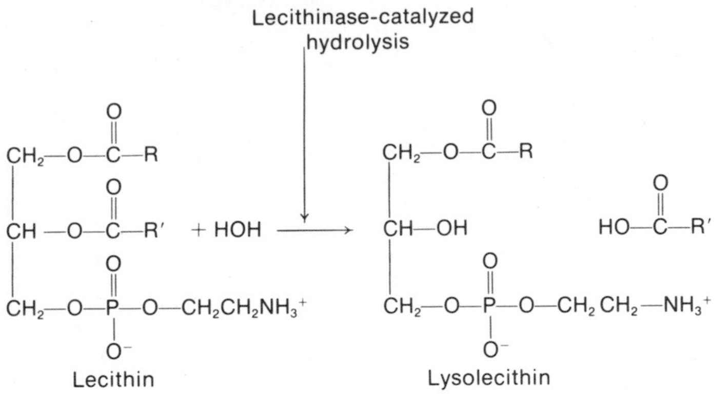

Lecithinase-catalyzed
hydrolysis

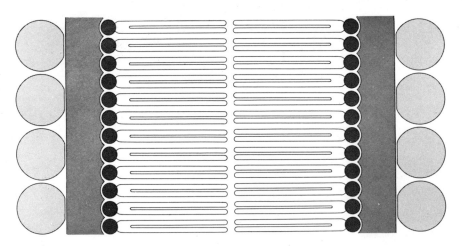

FIGURE 12.3.

Hydrolysis of a lecithin.

as the membrane structure disintegrates (see Figure 12.4). It is of vital interest to snake handlers that some snake venoms contain large amounts of lecithinase, which, upon injection into the blood stream, causes the same sort of cell disruption as you will observe in this experiment.

Take three test tubes, and add 0.5 ml of blood to each. Then add 10 ml of 0.95% NaCl (physiological saline) to one tube, and 10 ml of water to the second.

To the third tube, add 9 ml of saline and 1 ml of lecithinase solution. Note the results.

NOTES AND REVIEW QUESTIONS

1. Prepare a graph describing the relation of acid equivalents titrated to the time of incubation of substrate with lipase.

FIGURE 12.4.

"Butter sandwich" version of membrane structure is schematically represented. Two layers of lipids, their fatty tails pointing in and their water-soluble heads pointing out, make up the middle section. They lie between two thin sheets of protein (*medium gray bands*). These sheets of protein are thought to be coated with globular proteins (*light gray circles*). (From L. E. Hokin and M. R. Hokin, "The Chemistry of Cell Membranes." Copyright © 1965 by Scientific American, Inc. All rights reserved.)

2. Report the data of the pH electrode measurement in a table under the following headings: *time, ml of KOH added,* and *milliequivalents of KOH added.* Calculate the rate of enzymatic release of acid as milliequivalents of acid formed per minute.

3. Prepare a graph that describes the percentage bleaching of carotene as a function of time.

4. Describe the appearance of the blood samples, and interpret your observations.

REFERENCES

1. M. Bier, "Lipases," in S. P. Colowick and N. O. Kaplan, eds., *Methods in Enzymology,* (Academic Press, 1955), I, 627.

2. L. E. Hokin and M. R. Hokin, "The Chemistry of Cell Membranes," *Scientific American,* October 1965. Offprint No. 1022.

3. A. L. Tappel, "Lipoxidase," in S. P. Colowick and N. O. Kaplan, eds., *Methods in Enzymology,* (Academic Press, 1962), V, 539.

NUCLEIC ACIDS, THE BASIS OF BIOCHEMICAL IDENTITY

Models of Their Structure, Function, and Information-Carrying Role

This experiment, an exercise in model building, is intended to give you some three-dimensional sense of the coding and physical properties of nucleic acid molecules. Three of the major classes of nucleic acids are described by the models.

Transfer RNA (tRNA) is a small molecule whose biochemical activity can be measured in an *in vitro* enzymatic assay. Because it is small, and because its activity can be thus measured, pure transfer RNA has been isolated, and the sequence of its nucleotides has been established. Although the three-dimensional structure of tRNA is still being studied, Figure 13.1 shows a very probable approximation of its general structure. You will assemble foam-rubber symbols on wire to make a model of one species of transfer RNA.

With a simplified dictionary for the translation of amino acid positions into nucleotide triplet codons, you will assemble a short segment of *messenger RNA* (mRNA). In general, "to translate" is to convert an expression from the symbols of one language into the symbols of another language. Here you are translating the symbols of sequential amino acid arrangement into the symbols of sequential nucleotide arrangement.

Then, using the rules of complimentary base-pairing, you can transcribe the messenger RNA segment into a complimentary segment representing the same information as encoded on a structural gene. To transcribe is to rewrite in the same language, although one may often use different symbols, as in the transcription of shorthand notes into a polished typewritten record. Thus the nucleotide language is retained in the transcription of a DNA sequence into an RNA message.

You will make a three-dimensional model of DNA from wire and paper symbols to show the function of base-pairing in maintaining the structure of DNA and in allowing the duplication and expression of genes.

EXPERIMENTAL PROCEDURES

1. Transfer RNA

Assemble the foam-rubber models of nucleotides (see Figure 13.2) by piercing them at carbons 3 and 5 of adjacent ribose residues (the pentagons) with a tubing

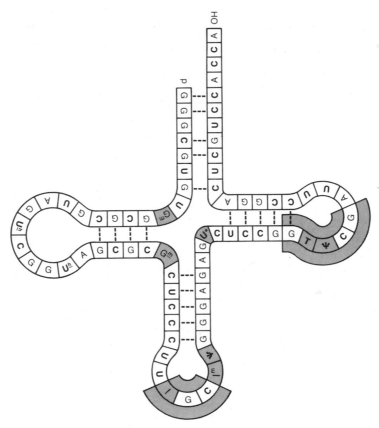

FIGURE 13.1.

Nucleotide sequence of a transfer RNA. (From R. W. Holley, "The Nucleotide Sequence of a Nucleic Acid." Copyright © 1966 by Scientific American, Inc. All rights reserved.)

spacer in between to represent the phosphodiester bridge (see Figure 13.3). Follow the sequence for the transfer RNA given in Figure 13.1, and then bend the model into the cloverleaf pattern shown by the figure. Note the relative positions of the amino acid carrying site and the coding site. Minor variations in the chemical structures of the bases are common in transfer RNA molecules. In following Figure 13.1, use: U for ψ, U^h, and U^*; G for G^m; and A for I and I^m.

2. Translation and Transcription

Assemble the messenger RNA for the decapeptide

> ser-ala-thr-arg-gly-glu-pro-asp-phe-his

from the foam-rubber nucleotides as before. Each amino acid is positioned by a messenger RNA template, in which a sequence of three nucleotides makes a symbol of recognition, or *codon,* for the appropriate amino acid. The problem of *degeneracy,* multiple

codons for positioning the same amino acid, will here be ignored for the sake of simplicity; use the "dictionary" given in Table 13.1 for translating amino acids into codons.

TABLE 13.1.

A Simplified Genetic Code.

Amino Acid	Codon	Amino Acid	Codon
ala	GCU	his	CAU
arg	CGG	phe	UUU
asp	GAU	pro	CCU
glu	GAA	ser	AGC
gly	GGU	thr	ACC

Be sure the codons are arranged in the sequence demanded by the given sequence of amino acids in the peptide. Now make a strand of DNA that is complementary to the strand of messenger RNA you have just made. Note that the role of thymine in DNA is

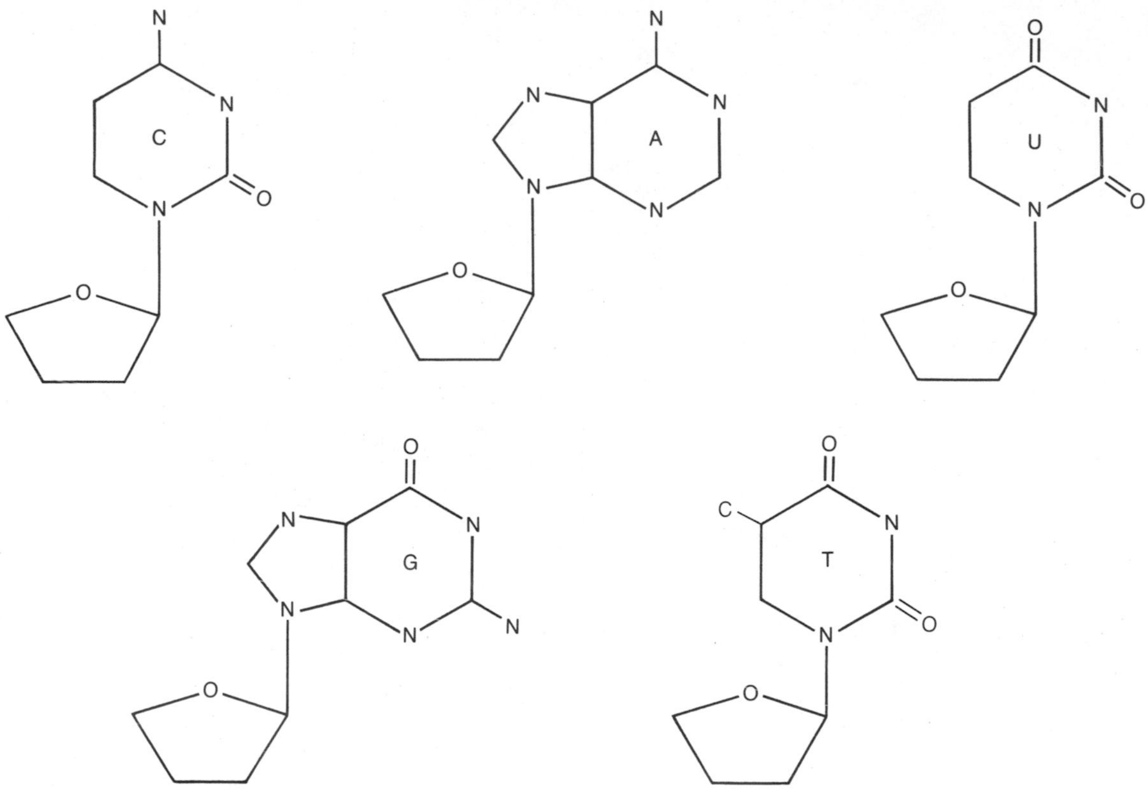

FIGURE 13.2.
Nucleotide symbols.

equivalent to the role of uracil in RNA. Table 13.2 shows the base-pairing between RNA and DNA that gives complementarity.

Have the RNA and DNA sequences checked by the instructor.

TABLE 13.2.
Nucleic Acid Base-Pairing.

RNA	DNA
A	T
G	C
U	A
C	G

3. The Double Helix

Get two 50-inch strands of No. 12 TW insulated, single-strand copper wire, of two different colors. On the instructor's bench there are several 50-inch lengths of masking tape crossmarked at intervals of 5/3 inches. Lay your strands of wire on this tape, and mark off the intervals on both wires with a wax pencil. These intervals will later mark the spacing for the base pairs.

Now bend each wire on the template (a 5-liter graduated cylinder, about 24 inches high and 4¼ inches wide), along the tape that has been wrapped around the cylinder. Make sure you coil the wire clockwise (as for a righthanded screw threading) to make an alpha helix, *not* a beta helix (see Experiment Two).

Next, get 30 pieces of small copper wire (No. 12 gauge) cut into six-inch lengths. Wrap both ends of each wire around a pencil point, about midway down the taper, to form a half-circle slightly larger than the diameter of your insulated wire. Now attach the short strands of copper wire to one of the helices by crimping one end closed with pliers at the wax-pencil marks.

Lay one helix on the desk and insert the second helix so that it is antiparallel to the first (see Figure

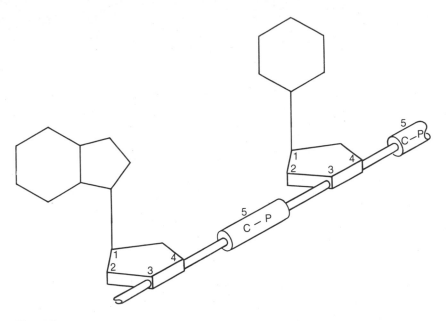

FIGURE 13.3.
Assembly of polynucleotide chain.

13.4). Then attach the free ends of the crosslinking wires to the free helix, starting at the first mark you made with the wax pencil. Be careful to keep the crosslinks in order; if you skip one, you will have to do much extra work in going back to put them in order. When you have linked all the wires, adjust the shape of the helices so that the crosslinks are perpendicular to the vertical axis of the double helix. The instructor will provide you with small cards that represent the hydrogen-bonded base-pairs (see Figure 13.5). Choosing one strand as the structural gene that coded your messenger RNA in part 2, tape the base-pairs to the crosswires in a sequence corresponding to the hereditary basis for the decapeptide sequence. The one strand is the structural gene; the other contains the information that could be used to direct the formation of a new structural gene. In protein synthesis, the strands separate; ribonucleotides are aligned by complimentary base-pairing with the structural gene strand, and then are stitched together to give the messenger RNA. You would need to cut the model in half across the hydrogen bonds to start this. To duplicate the hereditary information, the strands separate, and both strands act as templates for the alignment of deoxyribonucleotides by complimentary base-pairing to form two new double strands, one for each of the two cells that arise from the division of one cell. The elucidation of the structure of DNA is one of the very great achievements of science, since it

provides a clear basis for understanding the biological processes that depend on the structure of this molecule. You may keep the double-helix model to aid your further study of DNA and to provide your room with a contemporary ornament. Note that the model is about 40,000,000 times larger than life-size, and that the length of DNA needed to code for, say, a hemoglobin chain is 15 times as long.

NOTES AND REVIEW QUESTIONS

1. Make a table with four vertical columns and fifteen horizontal lines. The column headings are (1) amino acids, (2) mRNA codon, (3) DNA template, and (4) DNA opposite strand. On lines 2, 5, 8, 11, and 14 of the first column, write ser, arg, glu, phe, and asp to represent the sequence of a pentapeptide you have discovered. Fill in the next three columns, putting one letter on each line, and using the information given in this assignment.

2. In chromosome replication preceding cell division, what is the function of the DNA opposite strand described by column (4) of your table?

3. Judging by Charles Darwin's theory of biological evolution, if you isolated DNA from some animal tissue, would you be likely to find by X-ray analysis a beta helix (that is, one that turns counterclockwise)?

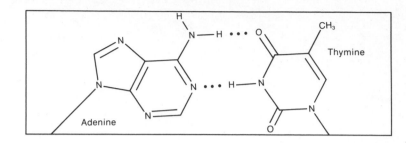

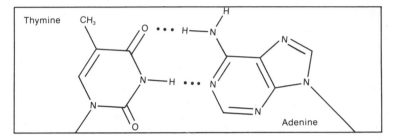

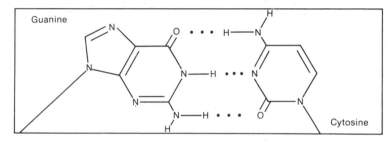

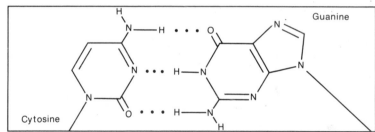

FIGURE 13.5.

Symbols for bases.

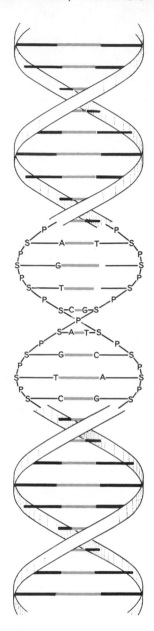

FIGURE 13.4.

DNA molecule is a double helix, diagramed here schematically. (One strand is actually displaced along the axis of the helix with regard to the other.) The backbone strands are composed of alternating sugar (S) and phosphate (P) groups. Attached to each sugar is one of four bases, usually adenine (A), guanine (G), thymine (T) and cytosine (C). Hydrogen bonds (gray) between bases link the strands. Adenine is always paired with thymine, guanine with cytosine. Genetic information is provided by the sequence of bases along a strand. (From R. A. Deering, "Ultraviolet Radiation and Nucleic Acid." Copyright © 1962 by Scientific American, Inc. All rights reserved.)

REFERENCES

1. F. H. C. Crick, "The Genetic Code: III," *Scientific American,* October 1966. Offprint No. 1052.
2. ———, "The Structure of the Hereditary Material," *Scientific American,* October 1954. Offprint No. 5.
3. R. W. Holley, "The Nucleotide Sequence of a Nucleic Acid," *Scientific American,* February 1966. Offprint No. 1033.
4. M. W. Nirenberg, "The Genetic Code: II," *Scientific American,* March 1963. Offprint No. 153.

NUCLEIC ACIDS

Isolation, Physical and Chemical Characterization, and Enzymatic Degradation

The experimental manipulation of deoxyribonucleic acid, DNA, will illustrate some of its physical and chemical characteristics. The DNA to be used in this experiment was isolated from calf thymus glands, the tissue of which is particularly rich in DNA. The isolation procedure begins with soaking the minced tissue in a concentrated solution of the detergent sodium dodecyl sulfate to strip the proteins (histones and protamines) from the nucleoprotein complex, leaving free DNA. The solution is next extracted with phenol to remove denatured protein and lipid. Next, the insolubility of DNA in ethanol and its solubility in salt solutions is used for purification. Addition of ethanol to the phenol-extracted DNA solution precipitates the DNA macromolecule. The precipitated DNA is then dissolved in salt solution. The cycle of ethanol precipitation followed by dissolving the DNA in salt solution is repeated twice more to remove impurities, and yields a sticky fibrous DNA product.

You will precipitate DNA molecules from solution by adding either ethanol or protamine sulfate. The precipitate is viscous because its long, stiff molecules stick together. The ethanol and protamine methods of precipitation are regularly used to purify DNA.

Diphenylamine is used as a specific coloring reagent for measurement of DNA. You will test the specificity of diphenylamine, showing that it reacts with deoxyribose but not with other sugars. A standard curve will relate the amount of diphenylamine-produced color to the amount of DNA present in the sample, showing that this reaction may be used as a quantitative measure of DNA concentration.

The viscosity of a DNA solution can be used to find out how many of the double strands of the molecules are intact; the double strands are rigid and make for a high viscosity in solution, whereas single-strand chains lack rigidity and give a low viscosity in solution. When the temperature of a DNA solution is carefully raised above a critical point, the interaction between base-pairs is interrupted, the double-stranded chains separate, and the viscosity falls. You will observe this change in physical property by measuring the viscosity of DNA samples at various temperatures.

You will measure the enzymatic degradation of DNA, first by measuring the drop in viscosity when deoxyribonuclease cleaves the long strands of DNA into short fragments. You will notice that very little terminal phosphate is released from DNA by a phosphatase (phosphomonoesterase), since there are few free ends of these molecules. Enzymatic release of phosphate can be greatly increased by deoxyribonuclease attack, which, by cleaving the chains into short lengths, exposes many new end-groups.

EXPERIMENTAL PROCEDURES

1. Precipitation of DNA by Ethanol and by Protamine Sulfate

As noted above, ethanol is used in the isolation of DNA because it readily precipitates the nucleic acid from solution. Another agent frequently used for the same purpose is protamine sulfate. Place 5.0 ml of DNA solution in a test tube. Slowly add ethanol while gently mixing the solution with a stirring rod. (Do *not* stir rapidly, since doing so will shear the long molecules into short segments.) As more ethanol is added, the solution becomes cloudy. Then, at the critical concentration of ethanol, DNA begins to come out of solution, in the form of strands that wrap themselves about the stirring rod. Save this DNA for part 2. Repeat the above procedure, this time using protamine sulfate instead of ethanol to precipitate the DNA.

2. Diphenylamine Assay

During the preparation of DNA, it would be advantageous to be able to measure the amount of DNA isolated. Since DNA might not be the only nucleic acid present (RNA is sometimes a contaminant), it is necessary to have a specific assay. Diphenylamine, when dissolved in glacial acetic acid and sulfuric acid, will react specifically with 2-deoxypentoses. The final product is blue, and can be measured exactly by recording its absorbance at 660 nm. Since deoxypentose is a major component of DNA, DNA is readily assayed in this manner.

The specificity of the diphenylamine assay is established as follows. Place 3.0 ml of each of the following solutions in separate test tubes: hexose, deoxyhexose, pentose, and 2-deoxypentose. Add 6.0 ml of diphenylamine reagent from a burette (CAUTION: it burns) to each tube, and heat the tubes in a boiling water bath for 10 minutes. Observe and record the color of the solutions after this treatment.

Suspend the DNA that was precipitated in part 1 in 5.0 ml of 10% trichloroacetic acid from a burette

(CAUTION: causes severe burns). Heat the suspension for 15 minutes in a water bath at 90 to 95°C. Take 1.0 ml of this suspension, add 2.0 ml of water, and then add 6.0 ml of diphenylamine reagent (CAUTION: burns). Set up four tubes for a standard curve as shown in Table 14.1. Heat all the test tubes in a boil-

TABLE 14.1.
Diphenylamine Standard Curve.

Add	Tube No.			
	1	2	3	4
DNA standard (1 mg/ml)	0.0[a]	0.2	0.5	1.0
Water	3.0	2.8	2.5	2.0
Diphenylamine reagent	6.0	6.0	6.0	6.0

[a] Units are ml.

ing water bath for 10 minutes. Cool the tubes to room temperature, and read their absorbances at 660 nm. Later you will plot absorbance against concentration of the standard DNA. You can then use this standard curve to calculate the amount of DNA precipitated in part 1. Carefully discard the contents of these tubes in a sink with water running.

3. Temperature Denaturation and the Melting Curve of DNA

Place 5.0 ml of DNA solution in each of six test tubes. Keep one of these tubes at each of the following temperatures for one hour: 0°, 25°, 65°, 80°, 90°, and 100°C; cap the ones at higher temperatures with marbles to prevent evaporation. At the end of the hour, cool the tubes, and measure and record the viscosity of each sample. The viscosity of each sample can be measured by recording the time required for the fluid level to fall through a fixed distance in a pipette. Make and average three measurements for each sample. Later, plot the viscosity of the sample against the temperature of preincubation.

4. Enzymatic Hydrolysis of DNA

During enzymatic hydrolysis by deoxyribonuclease (DNAase), it is the sugar-phosphate backbone of the DNA that is attacked. The enzyme hydrolyzes at random points the bonds between the sugar and the phosphate (see Figure 14.1). This attack produces many short, double-stranded segments of DNA. These seg-

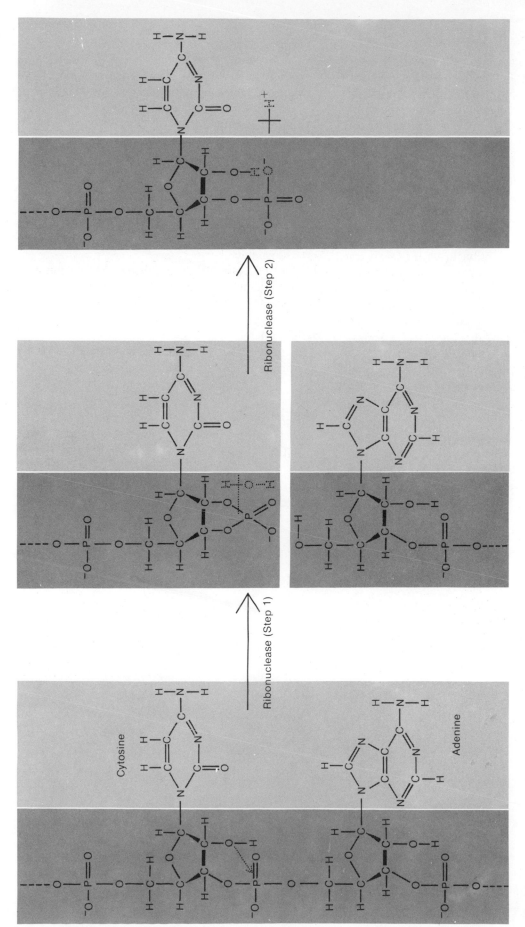

FIGURE 14.1.

Splitting of ribonucleic acid molecule by ribonuclease takes place in two steps. Backbone of the molecule, of which a segment is shown in dark shaded area, is attacked at the phosphorus atom following cytosine (or uracil) but not adenine (or guanine). In the first step the bond between phosphorous and the oxygen atom below it opens, splitting the molecule, a different oxygen uniting with the phosphorous (*dashed arrow*). In second step another phosphorus-oxygen bond is cleaved, with addition of water (H-O-H). (From W. H. Stein and S. Moore, "The Chemical Structure of Proteins." Copyright © 1961 by Scientific American, Inc. All rights reserved.)

ments can no longer give high viscosity to the solution. Place 5.0 ml of DNA solution in a test tube. In another tube, place 5.0 ml of 0.1M acetate buffer. Compare their viscosities (measuring each three times, and averaging). Add 0.2 ml of deoxyribonuclease solution to the tube containing DNA. Measure and record the viscosity every two minutes during a ten-minute period.

5. Action of Phosphate on DNA.

Place 5.0 ml of DNA solution in each of two test tubes. To one tube, add 1.0 ml of DNAase; to the other, add 0.5 ml of phosphatase. After 10 minutes, add 0.5 ml of phosphatase to the tube containing DNAase. After another 5 minutes, transfer a 3.0-ml aliquot from each to a new tube, and add 2.5 ml of phosphate-stopping reagent and 3.5 ml of water to each new tube. Allow 20 minutes for color development. Measure and record the absorbance at 620 nm.

NOTES AND REVIEW QUESTIONS

1. By referring to your text, to your general knowledge, or to any other reliable source, give a brief explanation of why ethanol and protamine sulfate cause DNA to precipitate.

2. Using the data from the diphenylamine assays, plot absorbance against the concentration of the standard DNA solution. Using this standard curve, calculate the amount of DNA obtained as a precipitate in part 1.

3. Plot viscosity (here as the drainage time in seconds of a constant volume from a pipette) against the temperature of preincubation. The T_m or melting point of a DNA sample is the temperature at the midpoint of the steep drop in viscosity when the strands are separating. Would you expect the T_m to depend on the base composition of the nucleic acid sample? Why?

4. Does DNAase attack its substrate at one end only or randomly along the length of the strand? Which method of attack would give a more rapid drop in viscosity?

5. Record the results from part 5. Explain, with a diagram, the results of this experiment in terms of enzyme specificity and substrate structure.

REFERENCES

1. D. Cantoni, "Preparation of DNA from Calf Thymus," in D. Cantoni and D. R. Davis, eds., *Procedures in Nucleic Acid Research* (Harper and Row, 1967).
2. S. Spiegelman, "Hybrid Nucleic Acids," *Scientific American*, May 1964. Offprint No. 183.

ENZYME INDUCTION

An Example of Controlled Gene Expression In Bacteria

Bacteria can make use of many different substrates that may turn up in their environment. In order to be used, each such substrate must be converted, by one or more unique enzymes, into some common metabolic intermediate that the bacteria can assimilate. Instead of synthesizing all possible enzymes for all possible substrates at all times, bacteria have learned to switch the synthesis of each enzyme on and off, the switching being triggered by the presence of the specific substrate for that enzyme. When a new substrate enters the cell, it interacts and combines with a regulatory protein called a repressor, which then can no longer prevent certain specific genes from expressing themselves. The newly derepressed genes direct the synthesis of a messenger RNA, which in turn directs the synthesis of enzymes that metabolize the substrate. When the substrate is all consumed, the repressor is freed of its combination with the substrate and again represses the function of those specific genes. As the cells continue to divide, the induced enzyme is diluted out by growth and its activity disappears from the culture. (See Figure 15.1.)

Much of what we know about enzyme induction is based on the enzyme beta-galactosidase in the bacterium Eschericia coli. This enzyme catalyzes the hydrolysis of beta-galactosides, such as the disaccharide lactose, releasing the monosaccharides for metabolic consumption. The enzyme is absent from cells grown in the absence of beta-galactoside, but appears rapidly when the latter is added to the culture medium. You will demonstrate the induction of beta-galactosidase by adding lactose to a culture of E. coli grown on glycerol. You will measure the induction of beta-galactosidase by a "gratuitous" inducer (one that induces the enzyme, yet is not a substrate for it), methyl-B-D-thiogalactopyranoside (TMG). You will observe that glucose inhibits the induction caused by lactose (called catabolite repression). You can demonstrate that the increase in beta-galactosidase activity results from synthesis of new enzyme protein, by attempting

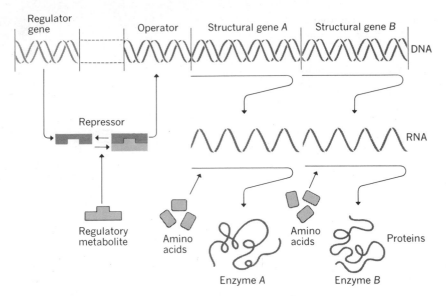

FIGURE 15.1.

Control of protein synthesis by a genetic "repressor" was proposed by François Jacob and Jacques Monod. A regulatory gene directs the synthesis of a molecule, the repressor, that binds a metabolite acting as a regulatory signal. This binding either activates or inactivates the repressor, depending on whether the system is "repressible" or "inducible." In its active state the repressor binds the genetic "operator," thereby causing it to switch off the structural genes that direct the synthesis of the enzymes. (From J. Changeux, "The Control of Biochemical Reactions." Copyright © 1965 by Scientific American, Inc. All rights reserved.)

to induce beta-galactosidase in the presence of chloramphenicol (CAP), which inhibits the function of the ribosomes in protein synthesis.

EXPERIMENTAL PROCEDURE

Since this is a complex series of experiments, requiring many measurements in rapid succession, you will have to work in pairs. Each pair of students will be given five 250-ml Erlenmeyer flasks, each containing 50 ml of a culture of E. coli. Make sure you have two ice buckets filled with ice. Then follow the procedure as enumerated below.

1. Take 20 large test tubes and put 4 drops of toluene in each one. The aliquots of variously induced cells will be placed in these tubes.
2. Label the five Erlenmeyer flasks A through E. Label the 20 tubes so that you have four test tubes for each flask (A1 through A4, B1 through B4, etc.).
3. To flask A, add 2 ml of water. Your partner will then immediately withdraw 4 ml of the mixture, and pipette it into the tube labeled A1. Urge your partner to pipette carefully; CAP is a toxic drug. He will then place the test tube in the ice and the

A flask in the 37° shaker to incubate. Note the time. You must place the test tube in ice, and you must note the time of withdrawal of this first sample. This will be your zero-time sample.

4. Repeat the procedure with flasks B through E, and tubes B1, C1, etc., but making the additions summarized in Table 15.1 instead of adding the 2.0 ml of water. You should be able to make these initial additions to and withdrawals from all five flasks within 10 minutes, and have all the flasks incubating at 37°C. *Remember to note the time of the first withdrawal from each flask.*

TABLE 15.1.

E. Coli Cultures.

Add	Flask				
	A	B	C	D	E
0.1M Lactose	0.0[a]	0.5	0.5	—	—
0.1M Glucose	—	—	1.0	—	—
Water	2.0	1.5	0.5	1.0	—
0.5M TMG	—	—	—	1.0	1.0
CAP (2.5 mg per ml)	—	—	—	—	1.0

[a] Units are ml.

5. At 10, 20, and 30 minutes, remove another 4-ml sample from each of the flasks. Pipette each sample into a test tube containing toluene, and place the tube in ice. The toluene will stop the induction and release the enzyme from the cell. The low temperature of the ice will stop all chemical activity, so that all the tubes may be conveniently assayed together.

6. After all the samples have been taken, you must assay all the tubes for beta-galactosidase activity to obtain a time course of induction. The assay is rather complicated but is accomplished as follows:

   a. Place all the sample tubes in a 37°C bath for 30 minutes.
   b. Add 0.4 ml of 0.01M orthonitrophenyl galactoside to each tube, your partner noting each time exactly. Keep the tubes at 37°C. As soon as a clearly visible yellow color develops, add 1 ml of 1M Na$_2$CO$_3$ from a burette to stop the reaction and again note the time exactly. The difference between these two times is the *incubation* time for that tube.
   c. Prepare a blank as follows. Take 4 ml of the mixture now in flask A and transfer it to a test tube. Add 4 drops of toluene, 1 ml of Na$_2$CO$_3$, and 0.4 ml of orthonitrophenyl galactoside, and mix well. Use this blank to set the colorimeter to zero at 420 and 550 nm.
   d. Read the absorbances of the tubes at 420 nm and at 550 nm. The reading at 550 nm is to correct for the turbidity of the bacteria. Remember to recalibrate the instrument to zero at each wavelength before reading.

NOTES AND REVIEW QUESTIONS

An absorbance of 0.0075 at 420 nm corresponds to the hydrolysis of 1 millimicromole (1mμmole) of orthonitrophenyl galactoside. Correct your reading at 420 nm by multiplying the absorbance at 550 nm by 1.65, and subtracting this value from the reading at 420 nm. Use the corrected absorbance to calculate the number of units of enzyme present. An enzyme unit is defined as the amount of enzyme that hydrolyzes 1 mμmole of orthonitrophenyl galactoside during one minute of the incubation for the assay (step 6b). Develop your data in tabular form, as below.

Flask	Induction time	*a* Incubation time	*b* A$_{420}$	*c* A$_{550}$	*d* A$_{550}$ ×1.65	*e* b−d	*f* Δ A$_{420}$/min. e/a	Enzyme units f/0.0075

Prepare a graph of enzyme units measured against time, for each flask, and interpret the results.

REFERENCES

1. J.-P. Changeux, "The Control of Biochemical Reactions," *Scientific American*, April 1965. Offprint No. 1008.
2. G. N. Cohen, *The Regulation of Cell Metabolism* (Holt, Rinehart, and Winston, 1968).

BIOCHEMICAL DIFFERENTIATION

Chemical Regulation and Expression of Cell Development in Complex Organisms

The development of higher organisms, from fertilized egg to mature adult, involves a series of obvious and very complex changes that are based on biochemical events. The induction of a bacterial enzyme by the appearance of a new substrate in the environment is a relatively simple example of how a biochemical event is controlled. In higher organisms, the controlling mechanisms and the resulting expressions of biochemical change are usually more complex. In the parts of this experiment, you will look at some biochemical expressions of cell differentiation or development. A plant growing from seed that has germinated in darkness will turn green in the light. This is an expression of the light-induced synthesis of chlorophyll and chloroplasts, which provide the plant with the ability to perform photosynthesis. Another type of control by light, operating through the phytochrome system rather than through chlorophyll, regulates the appearance of the enzyme inorganic pyrophosphatase in corn. The development of respiratory activity and of functioning mitochondria in seeds is triggered by water uptake when the seed germinates. The enzymes that break down reserve carbohydrates in seeds are

under similar control, although here a hormone-mediated step is recognized. In mammals, the amounts of numerous enzymes can be altered by administration of specific substrates and/or hormones. Rat-liver tryptophan pyrolase is increased by injection of either its substrate or a hormone.

EXPERIMENTAL PROCEDURES

1. Light-Dependent Chlorophyll Synthesis

Higher plants need light in order to complete the synthesis of chlorophyll. In fact, the appearance of many enzymes of photosynthesis and the assembly of the chloroplast structure—are triggered by illumination.

Four flats of seedlings will be available; all will have been germinated and kept in darkness until two days ago. One flat will have been brought into the light 48 hours before class; the second 24 hours before class; the third 12 hours before class; and the last left in darkness until class time. Take ten leaves from each flat, and put them in 25-ml beakers labeled 48, 24, 12, and 0 to identify their respective periods of illumination. Add 10 ml of 80% aqueous acetone from the burette, and crush the leaves in the beakers as thoroughly as possible with a small test tube. The acetone will denature the protein and dissolve the chlorophyll. Now filter the solution from each beaker into an appropriately labeled test tube, and measure and record the absorbance of each sample at 660 nm in the colorimeter. These values for chlorophyll concentration quantify the obvious greening of illuminated leaves, and they could be related to the appearance of CO_2 fixing ability, of Hill reaction, of photophosphorylation activity—that is, to the appearance of the plant's ability to perform photosynthesis.

2. Phytochrome-Triggered Appearance of Pyrophosphatase

In addition to the induction of the photosynthetic apparatus, light plays another regulatory role in plants. The germination of some seeds, the ripening of certain fruits, the appearance of such flowers as poinsettia and chrysanthemum—these and many other developmental characteristics of plants are controlled by light, but separately from the processes of photosynthesis. Instead of chlorphyll, a pigment called phytochrome "perceives" light and triggers the developmental processes (see Figures 16.1 and 16.2). The enzyme inorganic pyrophosphatase is formed in corn leaves when light activates the phytochrome system.

There will be two flats of corn seedlings available. Both will have been germinated six days ago. The control flat will have been kept in continuous darkness, whereas the irradiated seedlings will have been exposed, two days ago, to light from a 150-watt incandescent bulb for 10 minutes. Take the leaves of five seedlings from each flat for your two samples. Grind each sample with about half a teaspoonful of fine sand and 10 ml of .05M Tris buffer (pH 7.5). Filter each sample into a test tube, label it, and keep it on ice. Taking 1-ml aliquots from each sample, make a 1-in-10 and a 1-in-50 dilution of each sample with the Tris buffer solution, and keep them on ice also. Now label eight test tubes, and place in them the mixtures summarized in Table 16.1. Allow all the tubes to incubate for two minutes, then add 2.5 ml of the stopping reagent to each. After 10 minutes, read the tubes in the colorimeter at 620 nm, and record the absorbances.

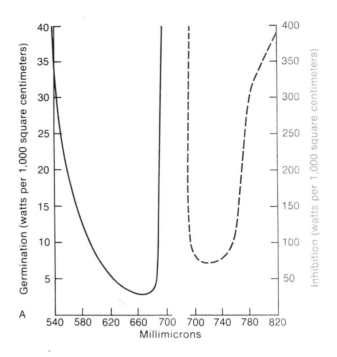

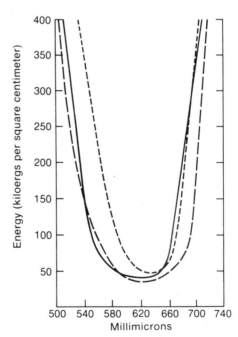

FIGURE 16.1.

Action spectra for the promotion (*left*) and inhibition (*middle*) of germination in lettuce seeds show energy of light required (*vertical scale*) at each wavelength (*horizontal scale*) to produce the desired effect in 50 per cent of the seeds. Curves at right are spectra for the promotion of flowering in barley (*solid line*), and for the inhibition of flowering in soybeans (*long dashes*) and cockleburs (*short dashes*). Barley flowers during short nights, and the other two flower when the nights are long. (From W. L. Butler and R. J. Downs, "Light and Plant Development." Copyright © 1960 by Scientific American, Inc. All rights reserved.)

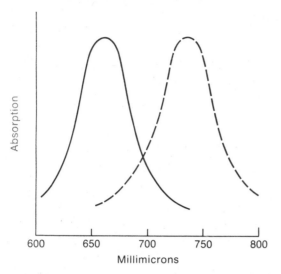

FIGURE 16.2.

Absorption spectra for the two forms of phytochrome are shown here. The form known as P_{660} (*solid line*) absorbs the most light at a wavelength of 660 millimicrons, while P_{735} (*broken line*) is far more absorbent, or opaque, to light at a wavelength of 735 millimicrons. The reactions of plants to these wavelengths indicate that P_{735} is the active form. (From W. L. Butler and R. J. Downs, "Light and Plant Development." Copyright © 1960 by Scientific American, Inc. All rights reserved.)

TABLE 16.1.

Inorganic Pyrophosphatase Assay.

Add	Tube No.							
	1	2	3	4	5	6	7	8
.001M Pyrophosphate	0.6[a]	0.6	0.6	—	0.6	0.6	0.6	—
.05M MgC1	0.2	0.2	0.2	0.2	0.2	0.2	0.2	0.2
Control sample,								
undiluted	0.2	—	—	0.2	—	—	—	—
diluted 1-in-10	—	0.2	—	—	—	—	—	—
diluted 1-in-50	—	—	0.2	—	—	—	—	—
Irradiated sample,								
undiluted	—	—	—	—	0.2	—	—	0.2
diluted 1-in-10	—	—	—	—	—	0.2	—	—
diluted 1-in-50	—	—	—	—	—	—	0.2	—

[a]Units are ml.

3. Development of Respiration in Germinating Seeds

The development of functional mitochondria and of respiratory activity in seeds is triggered by the uptake of water. Hydration of the seeds allows synthesis of the respiratory enzymes.

There will be five samples of soybeans available. All will have been soaked in water for six hours to initiate germination. Sample 1 will have been soaked during the six hours just before the class. Sample 2 will have been started 18 hours before and, after the six-hour soaking, the seeds will have been kept between wet towels. Sample 3 will have been started 24 hours before, and sample 4, 48 hours before, these also having been kept between wet towels. Sample 5 will have been treated like Sample 4, except that these seeds will have been in a solution containing 2.5 mg of chloramphenicol per ml of water instead of water alone. Place five seeds from each sample in 25-ml Erlenmeyer flasks, and, using a KOH trap, measure with a manometer the respiration activity during five minutes. Record the results for each sample.

4. Emergence of Phosphorylase Activity

Another manifestation of embryonic development within a germinating seed is the breakdown of carbohydrate reserves to supply the substrates for respiration and new cell growth. A convenient example of this process is found in barley seed, which synthesizes the enzyme amylase to degrade starch at an appropriate time after the beginning of germination.

Barley seeds will have been moistened by being kept between wet paper towels for 1, 12, 24, and 36 hours. Take eight seeds at each stage of germination, and grind the four samples separately with a mortar and pestle in 5 ml of 0.1M sodium acetate buffer (pH 5). Decant the soluble enzyme extracts into test tubes, then assay each extract for amylase activity. Amylase activity is measured by adding 1 ml of extract to 5 ml of a 1% starch solution. After a three-minute incubation, add one drop of iodine reagent. The addition of iodine reagent to a solution of starch produces a blue color, because the iodine is trapped in the helical coils of the starch chains. The color of the complex depends on the length of the helix, and becomes less blue as the helix is shortened (see Figure 16.3). An active amylase preparation will quickly cleave the starch helix into short segments that do not produce the blue color. Record your visual estimate of amylase activity.

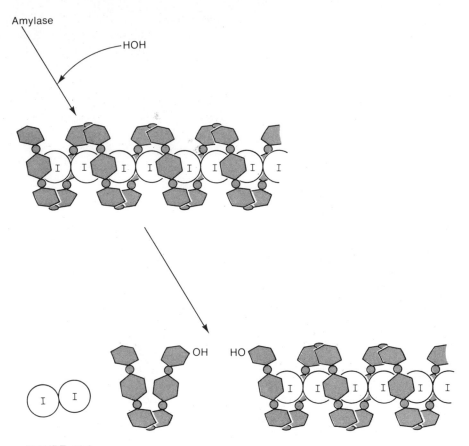

FIGURE 16.3.

Hydrolysis of a polysaccharide.

5. Hormonal Control of a Liver Enzyme

Tryptophan pyrolase is an enzyme in rat liver whose concentration can be controlled both by the amount of its substrate that is present and by hormones. Tryptophan pyrolase degrades tryptophan by catalyzing the reaction shown in Figure 16.4.

Glucocorticoid hormones, in general, stimulate glucose synthesis (gluconeogenesis) from various carbon skeletons, including the carbon skeletons of amino acids. Thus, many enzymes that degrade amino acids are induced or synthesized in greater amounts in response to a glucocorticoid injection. Such an injection increases both the synthesis of tryptophan pyrolase and the measurable activity of this enzyme in the liver. As a result of the increased enzyme activity, tryptophan is broken down to provide more carbon for glucose synthesis.

In another and independent control mechanism, the substrate of this enzyme, tryptophan, is able to increase the activity of the tryptophan pyrolase. Tryptophan prevents the normal destruction of tryptophan

pyrolase by the cells. Thus, an excess of substrate will protect the enzyme until the enzyme catalyzes the disappearance of the protective substrate.

Rats will have been subjected to the following procedure to provide the material for this part of the experiment. They were injected intraperitoneally with either 0.5 ml of physiological saline (0.9% NaCl) containing 1.25 mg cortisone for each 100 grams of body weight (see Figure 16.5), or with 1.82 ml of 5% L-tryptophan in saline per 100 grams of body weight, or with both cortisone and tryptophan in the same amounts. Five hours after injection, the enzyme changes are most pronounced. The rats were sacrificed, and the livers promptly removed, washed several times in ice water, and weighed to within 0.1 gram. Each liver was then homogenized in a Waring blender in seven volumes of cold 0.14M KCl containing 0.0025N NaOH. The homogenate was centrifuged at 800g for 10 minutes, or simply allowed to settle by standing in the cold.

This procedure provides four crude homogenates for enzyme assay: (1) from control rats, uninjected; (2) from rats injected with cortisone; (3) from rats

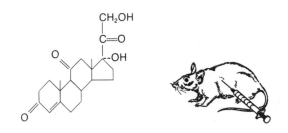

FIGURE 16.4.

Oxidative breakdown of tryptophan.

FIGURE 16.5.

The structure of cortisone.

injected with L-tryptophan; and (4) from rats injected with both cortisone and L-tryptophan.

To measure the activity of tryptophan pyrolase, one measures, with a spectrophotometer, how much kynurenine is formed during aerobic incubation of the liver homogenates with L-tryptophan. (The immediate oxidation product, formyl kynurenine, is not accumulated, because there is always much kynurenine formidase in the crude liver preparations.)

The reaction is carried out in 20-ml beakers. Prepare reaction mixtures in five numbered beakers as summarized in Table 16.2. Incubate the reaction mix-

tures in a shaker at 37°C for one hour after adding the homogenate. Then stop the reaction by adding 2 ml of 15% metaphosphoric acid (*Caution*: causes severe burns) from a burette. Filter the reaction mixtures to remove denatured protein. Adjust each filtrate to a *p*H of 6.5 to 7.5 by adding about 1.0 ml of 1.1*N* NaOH. Measure the absorbance of each neutralized solution against a water blank at 365 nm. Record the measured absorbance, which is proportional to the amount of kynurenine formed by tryptophan pyrolase.

NOTES AND REVIEW QUESTIONS

1. Prepare a graph describing the concentration of chlorophyll, as indicated by the absorbance at 660 nm plotted against the period of illumination of seedlings grown in the dark.
2. Report the data describing phytochrome-induced enzyme synthesis. What percentage increase in pyrophosphatase activity results from phytochrome photoactivation?
3. Prepare a graph relating measured respiratory activity to the length of development after germination. What was the percentage of inhibition by chloramphenicol?
4. Prepare a table describing the relation of amylase activity to length of time of barley-seed development.
5. Draw a bar graph to illustrate the effects of substrate and hormone injections on the tryptophan pyrolase activity of rat liver.

REFERENCES

1. R. Bernhard, "Enzymes—Their Ups and Downs in Animal Cells," *Scientific Research*, 4 (November 1969), 30.
2. L. Butler and V. Bennett, "Phytochrome Control of Maize Leaf Inorganic Pyrophosphatase," *Plant Physiology*, 44 (1969), 1285.
3. W. L. Butler and R. J. Downs, "Light and Plant Development," *Scientific American*, December 1960. Offprint No. 107.
4. R. T. Schimke *et al.*, "Biochemical and Biophysical Research," *Communication*, 15 (1964), 214.
5. J. E. Varner and G. Ram Chandra, "Hormonal Control of Enzyme Synthesis in Barley Endosperm," *Proceedings of the National Academy of Sciences of the United States of America*, 52 (1964), 100.

TABLE 16.2.

Kynurenine Assay.

	Beaker No.				
Add	1	2	3	4	5
0.2M phosphate buffer, pH 7	1.0[a]	1.0	1.0	1.0	1.0
0.2M L-tryptophan	0.3	0.3	0.3	0.3	—
Water	0.7	0.7	0.7	0.7	1.0
Homogenate number 1	2.0	—	—	—	—
2	—	2.0	—	—	—
3	—	—	2.0	—	—
4	—	—	—	2.0	2.0

[a]Units are ml.